Idries Shah was born in 1924 into a family that traces itself through the Prophet Mohammed to the Sasanian Emperors of Persia and, beyond that, back to the year 122 B.C.—perhaps the oldest recorded lineage on earth. Shah is the author of sixteen books published in five languages and forty-five editions throughout the world. Their subject matter ranges over travel, bibliography, literature, humor, philosophy, and history, but their author is most prominent for his writings on Sufi thought as it applies to the cultures of both East and West. Despite the extraordinary success of these books, Shah refuses newspaper interviews and declines to play the role of a "guru," preferring hard and silent work in his chosen milieu of thinkers and artists. He has recently been awarded the Dictionary of International Biography's Certificate of Merit for Distinguished Service to Human Thought. In addition to *Caravan of Dreams*, Penguin Books publishes Shah's *Reflections* and *Thinkers of the East*

Here we are, all of us: in a dream-caravan.
A caravan, but a dream—a dream, but a caravan.
And we know which are the dreams.
Therein lies the hope.
> —Our Teacher Bahaudin, *El Shah*

The Dog may bark, but the caravan moves on.
> —*Proverb*

IDRIES SHAH

CARAVAN
OF DREAMS

Penguin Books Inc
Baltimore · Maryland

Penguin Books Inc
7110 Ambassador Road
Baltimore, Maryland 21207, U.S.A.

First published by The Octagon Press, England 1968
Published in Penguin Books 1972

Printed in the United States of America by
Kingsport Press Inc, Kingsport, Tennessee

Library of Congress Catalog Card Number 71–171351

FOR
KASHFI, SAIRA, SAFIA
AND
TAHIR SHAH

Traditions of the Prophet from the Authentic Collections and Sufi traditional accounts. *The Tale of Melon City* from oral sources in Afghanistan. *Haughty and Generous* from a story-teller in Khanabad. *Definitions* from the Wisdom of Mulla Do-Piaza. *Adventures of Mulla Nasrudin* collected by the Author from oral sources. *Red Sea Journey* and *Pilgrimage to Mecca* from Destination Mecca, by Idries Shah. *Hospitality* from oral legend. *The Man the Snake and the Stone* from dervish recitals. *The Mongols* from the Table Talk of Khoja Anis. *The Magic Horse* from the Sarmuni Collection. *Sayings and Proverbs* collected by the Author. Baghdad and Spain from Gibbon's *Decline and Fall*. *The Prince of Darkness* and *The Man who cheated the Angel of Death* contributed by Amina Ali-Shah. *Mushkil Gusha* from story-tellers. Other extracts without attribution are original or widely found in folk-recitals.

NTS

PREFACE

IN one of the best tales of the *Arabian Nights*, Maruf the Cobbler found himself daydreaming his own fabulous caravan of riches.*

Destitute and almost friendless in an alien land, Maruf at first mentally conceived – and then described – an unbelievably valuable cargo on its way to him.

Instead of leading to exposure and disgrace, this idea was the foundation of his eventual success. The imagined caravan took shape, became real for a time – and arrived.

May your caravan of dreams, too, find its way to you.

IDRIES SHAH

---

* Retold in my *Tales of the Dervishes* (1967), pages 162–8.

Traditions of the Prophet

Traditions of the Prophet

MANY people will hardly believe that, although the words of virtually every other major teacher of human ideas are available in popular form, there is no general collection of the Traditions of the Prophet Mohammed in English, nor in any of the other Western languages, over 1,300 years after his time.

There are, of course, in Arabic and Persian, several received collections of Traditions, representing a colossal amount of labour in compilation, verification and transmission.

Statistics on record of the work of noteworthy traditionists are impressive even by modern standards. Over one hundred and seventy of the eminent traditionists of Islam were women. In making his authoritative collection the Imam Bokhari personally investigated and tested for accuracy against the testimony of witnesses 600,000 entries, of which he eventually selected as incontestably correct just over five thousand traditions.

Ibn Rustam spent the modern equivalent of more than a quarter of a million pounds on research into the accuracy of traditions; Abu Daud collected five thousand genuine sayings after twenty years' work. Asim Ibn Ali was a traditionist of such repute that he was known to have actual classes of 120,000 students. The manner of analysing traditions for accuracy developed into a science: Ibn Jauzi alone wrote 250 books on this subject.

The following selection represents a sample recorded by Baghawi of Herat, Afghanistan, author of the *Mishkat*, recognised as a standard work, by Tirmidhi, Rumi, Muslim, Bokhari and dervish collections in use throughout the East.

SAYINGS OF THE PROPHET

Trust
Trust in God – but tie your camel first.

The World
Treat this world as I do, like a wayfarer; like a horseman who stops in the shade of a tree for a time, and then moves on.

Objects
It is your attachment to objects which makes you blind and deaf.

Sleep
Sleep is the brother of death.

Reflection
The Faithful are mirrors, one to the other.

Women
Women are the twin-halves of men.

Privacy
Whoever invades people's privacy corrupts them.

Wives
A virtuous wife is the best treasure any man can have.

Oppression
When oppression exists, even the bird dies in its nest.

Love
Do you think you love your Creator? Love your fellow-creature first.

Distribution
God it is who gives: I am only a distributor.

Helping others
I order you to assist any oppressed person, whether he is a Moslem or not.

Monkishness
No monkery in Islam.

The Pious
My back has been broken by 'pious' men.

Cursing
You ask me to curse unbelievers. But I was not sent to curse.

Teaching
One hour's teaching is better than a whole night of prayer.

Day and Night
The night is long: do not shorten it by sleep. The day is fair: do not darken it with wrongdoing.

Humility
Humility and courtesy are themselves a part of piety.

Envy
Envy devours good deeds, as a fire devours fuel.

The learned
Whoever honours the learned, honours me.

Poverty
My poverty is my pride.

Death
Die before your death.

The Tongue
A man slips with his tongue more than with his feet.

Desire
Desire not the world, and God will love you. Desire not what others have, and they will love you.

Pride and Generosity
Pride in ancestry is really a property-interest. Generosity is a variety of piety.

Practise
Who are the learned? Those who put into practise what they know.

Kindness
Whoever has no kindness has no faith.

Princes and Scholars
The best of princes is one who visits the wise. The worst of scholars is one who visits princes.

Anger
You ask for a piece of advice. I tell you: 'Do not get angry.' He is strong who can withhold anger.

The Judge
A man appointed to be a judge has been killed without a knife.

Struggle
The holy warrior is him who struggles with himself.

Ink and Blood
The ink of the learned is holier than the blood of the martyr.

Contemplation
An hour's contemplation is better than a year's worship.

Understanding
Speak to everyone in accordance with his degree of understanding.

Food
Nobody has eaten better food than that won by his own labour.

Work
I am a worker.

Accusations
Anyone reviling a brother for a sin will not himself die before committing it.

Paradise
I will stand surety for Paradise if you save yourselves from six things: telling untruths, violating promises, dishonouring trust, being unchaste in thought and act, striking the first blow, taking what is bad and unlawful.

Tasks
Whoever makes all his tasks one task, God will help him in his other concerns.

Poetry
In some poetry there is wisdom.

Lies, promises, trust
He is not of mine who lies, breaks a promise or fails in his trust.

Thoughts
Good thoughts are a part of worship.

Vision of the Faithful
The Faithful see with the light of God.

Some behaviour
I am like a man who has lighted a fire, and all the creeping things have rushed to burn themselves in it.

The Koran
The Koran has been revealed in seven forms. Each verse has inner and outer meaning.

Obligation to Learn
The pursuit of knowledge is obligatory on every Moslem.

The Young in Paradise
Old women will not enter Paradise: they will be made young and beautiful first.

A Journey
On a journey, the lord of a people is their servant.

Recognition
Souls which recognise one another congregate together. Those which do not, argue with one another.

Truth
Speaking the truth to the unjust is the best of holy wars.

Knowledge
Journey even as far as China seeking knowledge.

The time will come
The time will come when you are divided into seventy-two sects. A group among you will be my people, the people of Salvation.

The Bequest
I have nothing to leave you except my family.

MOTIVES

The Messenger of Allah said:

A martyr will be brought before God on resurrection day and the man will say 'I fought for your cause, even to martyrdom.'

God will say: 'You are a liar. You fought in order that you should be called a hero, and people *have* called you such.'

He will be taken to hell.

Then a man learned in the Koran will be brought and he will say: 'I studied and read the Koran for Your sake.'

God will say: 'You are a liar. You gained learning, in order to be called learned by men. They *have* called you learned.'

He will be taken into Hell.

Now a rich man will be brought forward, and he will say: 'I have given liberally for that to which You desired generosity to be extended.'

'God will say. 'You are a liar. You did what you did in order to be called generous by men. They *have* called you generous.'

He will be taken into hell.

From the Mishkat

The bier of a Jew was carried past. The Messenger stood up in respect. Someone said: 'It is the body of a Jew.' The Prophet answered: 'Is it not a soul?'

Abu Musa records

The Prophet said: 'Feed the hungry, visit those who are sick, free the captive.'

If anyone seeks learning to argue with the wise or to dispute with the foolish, or to attract attention to himself, Allah will deliver him into hell.

Men will come from every part of this earth to understand the Faith. When they come to you, give them right advice.

Whoever is without gentleness is devoid of good.

Aisha relates

When given a choice, the Messenger always took the lesser of two objects.

The Emissary patched his own sandals, did his own work, behaved in the house like anyone else.

Abdulla son of Harith states
I have never seen anyone who smiled more than the Envoy of Allah.

Anas testifies
I never saw anyone more kind to children than the Messenger of God.

Mu'ad recalls
The last words I had from the Messenger were: 'Treat people well, Mu'ad.'

FIRST REVELATIONS OF THE KORAN

The Messenger's first communication was a vision which he had in his sleep. It was like the brightness of the dawn.

He used to go to the cave on Mount Hira for worship for some days, until the longing to see his family came to him. He took food with him to Hira.

The angel came to him there and said: 'Read!' and he said: 'I cannot read!' And this happened several times, with the angel squeezing him and repeating 'Read'.

The angel said:

> 'Read in the Name of your Lord, who made man from a clot. Read, for your most generous Lord is Who taught the use of the pen, Who taught man what he did not know!'

The Messenger returned in terror to his wife Khadija and said: 'Wrap me up, wrap me.'

He told her what had happened, and said: 'I have fear for myself.'

She said: 'It is not so! I swear by Allah that I will never betray you. You are known to be truthful and a bearer of the burdens of others. You give to the poor, you feed guests, you work against injustice.'

Khadija took the Messenger to Waraqa the Christian, son of Naufal, her cousin, and said: 'Listen to what your nephew has said that he saw.'

Waraqa said: 'Nephew, what have you seen?'

The Messenger told him what he had seen, and Waraqa answered:

'It is the same Message which God sent to Moses. If only I were to be young during your time of prophethood! Would that I could be there when they come to cast you out!'

The Messenger of Allah asked, 'Will they then cast me out?'

Waraqa said to him: 'They will. No man has ever brought the like of that which you have brought without being opposed. If I live during your mission, I will help you, with all my energy.'

THE DEPUTATION IN NEED

Jarir relates:

At dawn one day I was with others in the company of the Messenger. A party of people came to him, from the people of Mudar. They had hardly any clothes, and their swords were slung on their backs.

At the sight of their poverty the Messenger of God showed anger. He went into his house.

He came out soon afterwards and ordered Bilal to give the Call to Prayer.

After the devotions, the Prophet said in his sermon:

'Fear your Lord, people, he who created you all from one soul. God watches over you . . .

'Let charity be given, money, wheat, dates, even half a date.'

One of the Helpers brought money more than his hand could hold. Then came people with presents until there were two piles of food and of clothes. And the face of the Messenger shone as if it were made of gold.

He said: 'If a person starts a good tradition in Islam, he will be rewarded for so doing to the extent of the rewards of those who copy him, without their own reward being in any way reduced. And whoever establishes a bad precedent in Islam will bear the burden of it and of all who follow it, without their own burdens being reduced in any way.'

THE BURDEN OF ALI

Ali, the Caliph, reports:

The pagan embargo upon the believers in Mecca had reached the point of our utmost suffering. None, including women and children, was allowed by the pagan Keepers of the Shrine of Abraham to buy anything. Nobody in the city dared give us even a drop of water.

They came, when we were feeble, servants of the Koresh, under arms, to my house, to take away the Messenger.

I went to the door as they started to enter, with a large board on my head, covered by a cloth, and began to carry it past them.

One of the soldiers said:

'What have you on your head, O Ali?'

I answered, 'Upon my head, the Prophet of Allah, of course, whom you have come to kill!'

They laughed and went into the house. It was in this manner that Allah preserved his Messenger, and granted us the blessing of Islam. He was lying on the board on my head, covered by the cloth.

OBSERVATION

One day the Prophet had been speaking about the way in which people take things too literally, not bothering themselves to think.

A woman came into his presence and the Prophet asked her the name of her husband.

She said: 'Such-and-such a man.'

'Ah, the man whose eyes are mostly white?' asked Mohammad.

'Not at all,' said the woman, 'my husband has normal eyes.'

When she went home she told her husband that the Prophet had mistaken her for the wife of someone else.

'But had you not noticed,' said the man, 'that the greater part of anyone's eyeball *is* white?'

THAT DAY IN THE CAVE

Abu Bakr reports:

During the Flight to Medina, we were hiding in the cave that day when the searching soldiers came straight towards the entrance.

I said to the Prophet, 'O Messenger of Allah! If they look this way, we are lost.'

23

He answered at once: 'Do you think then that we are only two, Abu Bakr? A Third is with us: we will be saved.'

He taught me the Secret Recital.

Koreshite searchers stepped to the cave's mouth and were about to enter.

Then we heard one say, suddenly, to another:

'They cannot be in here. See, there is an extensive spider's web spun across the entrance. They would have had to break it, entering.'

They passed on, swearing to hunt us down and kill us.

But we were saved. We continued the hard journey northward across the desert.

THE PARABLE OF THE RAIN

The Prophet Mohammed said of his knowledge that it was like a heavy rain falling upon the earth.

One part of the earth received the rain, and from that nourishment and what was in the earth produced plants and life.

Another patch of ground, not far away, took the water and collected it, making it available for mankind to drink.

A third area of the earth neither accepted the rainwater to keep it, nor did it absorb it to produce herbage.

In the first stage, the ground takes and also gives.
In the second it takes and gives, but does not use it.
In the third, the land is unaffected by the rain, it neither takes nor uses, nor does it give.

THE SON OF A CAMEL

A man went to Mohammed and asked him for a camel.

'I will give you the child of a camel,' said the Prophet.

'How can the child of a camel bear the weight of a huge man such as me?' asked the man.

'Quite easily,' said the Prophet; 'I will grant your wish and mine. Have this fully-grown camel – is it not the son of a camel?'

KNOWLEDGE

The Prophet said: 'There will be a time when knowledge is absent.'

Ziad son of Labid said: 'How could knowledge become absent, when we repeat the Koran, and teach it to our children, and they will teach it to their children, until the day of requital?'

The Messenger answered: 'You amaze me, Ziad, for I thought that you were the chief of the learned of Medina. Do the Jews and the Christians not read the Torah and the Gospels without understanding anything of their real meaning?'

* * *

HE would break his teeth on a lettuce leaf.

Proverb.

To an ant, a drizzle is torrential rain.

Proverb.

Adventures of Mulla Nasrudin

Adventures of Mulla Nasrudin

INSTANT READING

A certain famous Fakir was claiming in the village that he could teach an illiterate person to read by a lightning technique.

Nasrudin stepped out of the crowd:

'Very well, teach me – now.'

The Fakir touched the Mulla's forehead, and said: 'Now go home immediately and read a book.'

Half an hour later Nasrudin was back in the market-place, clutching a book. The Fakir had gone on his way.

'Can you read now, Mulla?' the people asked him.

'Yes, I can read – but that is not the point. Where is that charlatan?'

'How can he be a charlatan if he has caused you to read without learning?'

'Because this book, which is authoritative, says: "All Fakirs are frauds".'

WIVES

Nasrudin belonged to a club called 'The Assembly of Those who are not Afraid of their Wives'.

One day the Chairman called the meeting to order in the customary manner, saying: 'O all you who are not afraid of your wives – be seated.'

All sat except the Mulla.

'What's the matter, Nasrudin – are you afraid of your wife?'

'I'm not afraid of her, but I can't sit down. She beat me so hard last night that I'm black and blue.'

FIRST MAKE SURE

Nasrudin was going through a forest when he saw Selim, another villager, lying in a glade. A lion had attacked him and carried off his head.

Reflectively, the Mulla went back to the village.

As he passed the door of Selim's house, Mrs Selim called out: 'Nasrudin, I haven't seen my husband for some time. Do you suppose all is well with him?'

'That might depend, Madam,' said Nasrudin, 'upon whether he left the house with his head on or not.'

OBVIOUS

'What is your house like inside?'

'Very nice, Mulla, but there is no sunshine in it.'

'Is there no sunshine anywhere near you?'

'Yes, the garden has plenty.'

'Then why don't you move the house into it?'

WAIT UNTIL IT GETS YOU

One day Nasrudin was carrying a plate of food to a needy man. A loutish joker tripped him up, and the Mulla lost his temper.

'For that,' he roared, 'something terrible will happen to you!'

This startled the joker, who tripped over a rock and twisted his ankle. Feeling sorry for himself and repentant too, at such immediate punishment, he called out: 'I am sorry, Nasrudin; but you see, I have had my deserts.'

'Not at all,' replied the Mulla smoothly, 'that must have been a requital for one of your lesser misdeeds. When *my* curse hits you, you will be in no fit state even to apologise.'

BACK TO FRONT

'Reasonable people always see things in the same way,' said the Khan of Samarkand to Nasrudin one day.

'That is just the trouble with "reasonable" people,' said

Nasrudin; 'they include at least some people who always see only one thing out of a potential two possibilities.'

The Khan called the divines and the philosophers to explain, but they thought Nasrudin was talking nonsense.

The next day Nasrudin rode through the town on a donkey in such a way that his face was towards its tail.

When he arrived at the palace where the Khan was sitting with his advisors, Nasrudin said:

'Would your Highness please ask these people what they have just seen?'

When asked, they all said: 'A man riding back-to-front on a donkey.'

'That is exactly my point,' said Nasrudin. 'The trouble with them all is that they did not notice that perhaps it was me who was right and the donkey the wrong way around.'

THE RICH MAN

'How I wish I could be really wealthy,' said Nasrudin to his cronies in the teahouse, 'like, say, Kara Mustafa the great lord, who has everything.'

'How strange that you should say that,' said the potter, 'because in my shop a few minutes ago Mustafa himself was saying how much he wished that he were a poor and simple man.'

'But that is only because he is rich already!' said Nasrudin; 'he has the wish and also knows the method of becoming poor. *I* only have the desire to be rich!'

TEACH US YOUR WISDOM

Nasrudin arrived at a village far from his own home, and found that his reputation as a great teacher had preceded him.

The villagers assembled and their spokesman said:

'Teach us your wisdom, great Nasrudin.'

'Very well,' said the Mulla, 'but first of all let me suggest something useful to you. Would you like that unsightly hill opposite the village removed, so that you might enjoy the cool breezes which it now interrupts?'

The villagers were delighted at the proposal.

'Now,' said Nasrudin, 'bring me a rope long enough to encircle the hill, with some left over.'

After months of weaving the villagers produced the rope.

'Just put the rope around the hill, lift it up and put it on my back, so that I can take it away,' said Nasrudin.

'This is ridiculous,' said the villagers, 'how can we lift a hill?'

'How can I carry it away unless you do?' asked Nasrudin.

'It is the same problem when you ask me to teach you my wisdom.'

HOW TO WIN

Nasrudin decided to set himself up as a holy man.

He chose a certain town and declared in public that the local sage was an ignoramus. He promised to prove it with one question, in the market-place the following day.

The sage, enraged, presented himself at the time suggested. All the townspeople were present.

'I will now ask this gentleman a question,' said Nasrudin to the assembly; 'and if he cannot answer it, you will know which of us is the fool.'

Turning to the holy man, who was deeply versed in the sacred tongue of Arabic, he said: 'Tell me, what does "Marafsh" mean?'

'I do not know,' said the sage, translating.

The people drove him out as an imposter.

As he saw him on his way on the road which led out of town, the holy man said: 'You tricked me.'

'How long have you been the resident sage in this town?' asked the Mulla.

'Thirty years,' quavered the sage.

'And the wisdom which you have taught these people is only how to be tricked?'

THE LAW IS THE LAW

Mulla Nasrudin studied law under a tutor.

Since he had no money to pay for his lessons, the arrangement was that he would pay his fees as soon as he won a case.

But Nasrudin did not practise as an advocate.

The Tutor took the Mulla to court.

Nasrudin said, when the complaint had been heard:

'Your honour. If I win the case, claiming that my tutor need not be paid – he will not get his money.

'If, on the other hand, I lose, I shall not have to pay him, because I will not have won a case yet: he will not get his money.'

'What other result is possible?' asked the confused judge.

'Case dismissed,' said Mulla Nasrudin.

LOST: ONE DONKEY

'O People!' shouted Nasrudin, running through the streets of his village, 'Know that I have lost my donkey. Anyone who brings it back will be given the donkey as a reward!'

'You must be mad,' said some spectators to this strange event.

'Not at all,' said Nasrudin; 'do you not know that the pleasure which you get when you find something lost is greater than the joy of possessing it?'

I EAT . . .

In a small caravanserai four travellers were sitting eating the food which they had brought for themselves for their journey.

'I always eat almond paste and coriander-seed cakes with sugar plums,' said the rich merchant.

'I eat oatmeal and honey mixed with dried mulberries,' said the soldier.

'I eat dried curds and pistacho nuts with apricot puree,' said the scholar.

Having said their pieces, they all looked towards Nasrudin.

'I never eat anything else than wheat, carefully mixed with wheat and salt, water and yeast, and then correctly baked,' said the Mulla, unrolling a scrap of bread.

Red Sea Journey

Red Sea Journey

OURS was not a pilgrim ship – not, at any rate, at first. Suez seemed as Suez so often seems: hot and dusty, built on a kind of slope, as punishing to the feet as the local taximen's demands are to the purse. Stamped deeply at the time in its hopes as well as by its street signs with an unmistakable military presence, it felt somehow uneasy, brooding.

I was now a pilgrim, heading southwards through the Canal and the Red Sea, bound for Jeddah, the main port of Saudi Arabia.

When he saw my visa, the passport officer shrugged to his colleague of the Customs. Pilgrims, it seemed from his remarks, never had anything much dutiable.

I wondered, as I always do, why there should be so much preoccupation about people leaving the country. I had paid – quite generously, I thought – for the privilege of having my baggage examined upon entering. But there it was, and the usual procedure would have to be followed.

It is difficult to say whether this unvarying ritual is naïve, kindly or even lax. But the fact that I had seen about twenty of my future travelling companions go through it meant that I was prepared.

Thus, when the Customs man fixed me with a penetrating gaze, I was not surprised to hear the exultant *Haa-Haa!* of his fellow, strategically stationed directly behind me – and calculated, it seemed, to cause the intending smuggler immediately to leap out of his skin with fear and confess all.

Having survived this, I walked up the gangplank into a smallish vessel, clean enough but somehow too all-metal for this broiling sun. When we got under way, I was to think of this, to reflect that if I felt discomfort at the unyielding character of a steel ship, how much more aching must have been the regret of people used to the generous movement of wooden walls, with the white canvas billowing out above.

Both the captain and the inevitably red-haired engineer were Scots; the crew hailed from various parts of the Valley of the Nile. The passengers seemed to be of every nation except Egypt.

As we started, the call to midday prayer sounded from the third-class and steerage, where the patient pilgrims sat. A peasant Turkoman in felt boots (he had walked almost all the way from Persia) stood leading the worshippers facing Meccawards. Only three, so far, were dressed in pilgrim white: Ahmed the Somali, his wife, and their six-year-old son Abdullah. On our own deck a Saudi Sheikh, a Syrian agronomist and two Turkish journalists had already made friends. An American, bound for Aden, read Sherlock Holmes and called for tea every half-hour. The incessant blurred rhythm of Arabic music haunted every corner of the deck; loud-speakers carried the Cairo radio programmes from dawn to dusk.

As we negotiated the chain of connected lakes which make up the Canal, two days' steaming brought about a complete change of mood aboard the ship. It was as if we were in another world: everything of Cairo had been forgotten. There were no smells, no teeming hordes of curious and idle lingerers, nothing but the throb of the engines and the white birds circling overhead. We were but four days from Jeddah now, from the land to see which some of us had walked for years, others, saved all their lives.

The first unusual event was the complete abandoning of all distinctions between first- and third-class passengers. Though they spent most of their time in their own part of the ship, all passengers mixed freely and made one another welcome. One, more pious, perhaps, than others, prevailed upon the radio officer to discontinue the relaying of music. Under awnings the faithful sat, prayed or read books.

The Westernised first-class travellers now paced the deck in flowing robes: the Syrian still watered his plants five times a day, and he was growing a beard. I, too, stopped shaving, because it would have been discourteous to appear before the King clean-shaven – if I was to see the King, that was.

The American complained that the puritanical Saudi Sheikh had thrown all playing cards overboard as 'inventions of the Devil'.

One might have said – if this were not a phrase with completely irrelevant associations – that we were reverting to type. This was the transition period. The women passengers formed a group of their own, under the presidency of the wife of one of the clerics of the Mecca Sanctuary, who was returning from a visit to her sister in Cairo. She coached them in the recitations and prayers to be used during the Pilgrimage, and spoke of the work that she was doing in social welfare and for the benefit of children in the southerly province, the Hejaz.

I seemed to be the person with the best grasp of English, and the American soon attached himself to me. He questioned me rather narrowly as to the motives for my journey, what I expected to get out of it, and the conditions of life in Saudi Arabia.

Eventually the American asked me to take him to Mecca. He would be allowed, he said, to land at Jeddah. This was not a forbidden city. Once there, it should be possible, though not easy, to get into Mecca. He was willing to pay all expenses. He was willing, even, to reimburse me for my trouble. But I had troubles enough, and I told him that I would like to do it, but that being on the Pilgrimage I could not be a party to such a deception. Was he a Moslem? He was not. 'In that case you would not get much benefit out of going to Mecca,' I said.

But he wanted to be the first American to go there. After all, Mecca was far more impenetrable than Tibet. He knew, he'd been to Tibet. 'Nothing to it,' he told me.

If he became a Moslem would he be able to get in? I told him it was possible, but it would take time and perseverance. It might take years before he were sufficiently trusted. Even then, a false move could mean death. It has happened before. I reminded him that times were even more difficult than when such men as Burton got through in disguise. Today you have to run the gauntlet of walkie-talkie apparatus, identity cards and pilgrim passports – plus having to know the rituals and ways of Islam.

Suspense, suppressed excitement, the feeling of a profound experience soon to come, throbbed in every pilgrim heart as we neared Jeddah. In the brilliant hardness of the early morning sunlight, Saudi Arabia was sighted.

For the first time, as the white-garbed faithful lined the rails, I heard the immemorial pilgrim chant, to be repeated again a thousand times during my stay there: '*Labbayk, Allahumma, Labbayk!*' ('We are here, O Lord, we are here!').

Gleaming whitely, coral-built beyond those treacherous reefs through which ships cannot pass to her quayside, Jeddah beckoned, and Mecca: only fifty miles eastward through the desert.

Amid the cheers of the crew and chanting of the first chapter of the Koran ('The Opening'), we got into small boats and were ferried to the jetties where annually upwards of a hundred thousand Moslems land, from Morocco, Java, and almost every Eastern country.

Even before we reached the shore, striking evidence of the contrasts in a changing East abounded. Perched within the harbour on coral outcrops, fishermen were angling for the food which makes up so much of the protein diet of Jeddah's poorer citizens.

Large hoardings, inscribed in Arabic, Indonesian and half a dozen other tongues, proclaimed: *Pilgrims, Saudi Arabia Welcomes You*. Bronzed and hefty porters, their girdled costumes unchanged since Abraham's day, unloaded a Pakistani ship to the strains of the traditional, haunting shanty of their trade. Stacked in immense heaps, merchandise from all the world lay awaiting Customs examination in the huge concrete buildings so new that the roofs were actually being put on while they were in active use. This was just a symptom of the age of plenty which multi-million dollar American oil royalties have brought to Arabia.

The Turkoman was already in tears as we landed, and spoke of the sand getting in his eyes as we shook hands in farewell.

Before Ibn Saud conquered this country, the peninsula was divided into the austere northern part – Nejd – and this, the southern, easy-going Hejaz. Even today, thirty years later, the King keeps his capital in Riyadh – towards the Persian Gulf – and foreign embassies accredited to Saudi Arabia must remain by law in Jeddah, dotted in their graceful mansions around the curving inland bay.

Each group of pilgrims went to the arched Hall of Pilgrim Reception, for refreshment, identification, and allocation of guides. I put my bags on the Customs bench, and opened them.

I had not expected any special treatment. But as soon as I

presented my passport, a gorgeously robed sheikh of the Administration of Hospitality took charge of me. I was ushered into a
modern American car, and driven rapidly through the dazzling
ultra-modern streets to the *Diafa*, guest-apartments of the King.

Entering the thickly carpeted, cool vastness of the hall of
reception, I felt some diffidence in giving my full name to the
manager. This white-robed figure, with the twin camel-hair
circlets of the bedouin on his head, I felt, might harbour some
antagonism towards descendants of the Prophet, on political
grounds. I knew that the Saudis would not permit any privileged
class, and expected some sort of adverse reaction. However this
may once have been, it is no longer the case.

I was announced to the assembled gathering with many a
high-flown title. Grave, bearded faces courteously composed, they
rose, and we kissed each other's hands.

When I got to the middle of the horseshoe of armchairs which
formed the assembly a giant, red-bearded elder noticed my
hesitation. 'I am the doctor in charge of the Quarantine,' he told
me, with an Edinburgh lilt to his excellent Arabic. Like all
foreigners in Saudi Arabia he wore the white robe and sand-brown
bedouin cloak woven from the hair of the Kuwait camel.

I was later to meet several such men: engineers, doctors,
scientists, from Britain, America, Czechoslovakia or France: Saudi
officials now, and remarkably confident in their adopted characters
of what are locally called *Musta' Arabin* – 'Arabised ones' – just as
Robert of Chester and Michael Scot were known as Musta' Arabi
in the Moorish Spain of an earlier age.

Upon reflection, it is hard to say why one should at first feel this
change to be so odd. Why should it be taken for granted that an
Arab may live in Britain as the British do, yet the reverse appear so
unusual or difficult?

I sent a radio-telegram to the King at Riyadh, announcing my
arrival, and stating that I was ready to fly to the capital to render
him homage, after performing my essential Pilgrimage duties in
the Holy City.

The new Post Office building where I sent this message was an
eye-opener. Today's Arab buildings in Jeddah are built in a
blending of the ancient and Western styles, and equipped with what

41

seems a complete disregard for expense. Faisal Street (named after King Faisal, formerly the Viceroy of the Hejaz) runs through the centre of the new town, right up to the docks. And this, at the other end of the city, joins the Pilgrim Way, the newly macadamed road leading to Mecca itself.

Dominated on both sides by immense steel and concrete structures – apartment-houses, banks and administrative buildings – fish-tailed Cadillacs purr through its sweeping length. You will not find many places like Jeddah in the Middle East. Yet, in spite of an almost bewildering array of Western products and machines, Jeddah still holds much of that indefinable quality which even sociologists cannot analyse, and today we must still call the magic of the East.

Dressed in my one-piece, unstitched robe of cotton, with sandalled feet, with bare head in a temperature of 113 degrees Fahrenheit, I wandered farther afield. This is the obligatory garb of all who come to make the Pilgrimage. None may wear silk nor anything that would show social distinctions.

The town's cosmopolitan cafés, although they serve Western soft drinks as well as the harsh Nejdi coffee, do not cater for any superficially Westernised clientele. Although the fierce-eyed, armed-to-the-teeth bedouin from the desert does stand out in contrast with his more sophisticated urban compatriot, yet, for all this, both the well-trained Arab radio engineer or oil technician, and the tribesman from the wilds, continue to conform to age-old tradition: the code which increasing prosperity only seems to make more binding. This is probably because the Royal Family set the fashion.

The historic headcloth, bound with interlinked ropes, and a voluminous camel hair cloak, remain their common heritage. The advent of newspapers and the radio, indeed, actually appear to have increased the Arab's innate appreciation of his own way of life. This is one of the most striking things about Saudi Arabia today. Unlike the people of so many Eastern lands, the Saudis really feel that they are on a basis of equality with everyone else. That is why they do not ape the West in much detail.

King Abdul-Aziz Ibn Saud, in his modernisation programme, had to combat a very natural reluctance on the part of the more conservative elements to welcome people and machines which they did not fully understand. Just after the First World War, be it remembered, a dozen Arab nations were under Colonial or quasi-Colonial rule.

On the other hand, the real nomad of the desert has always been free. Secure in the wilderness of the sands, following desert tracks known only to himself, he has completely escaped that fear of the interloper which haunted settled townsmen. It is from the ranks of the bedouin, therefore, that come the country's new doctors, pilots, mechanics and technicians.

Beyond the British Embassy in Jeddah lie the ancient many-storied mansions of the merchant princes, their delicately carved rosewood lattices ajar to capture any fugitive breeze. Evidence of the invigorating role of oil royalties rises on every side, everywhere. Hawk-eyed bedouin chiefs drive cars of such modernity that I had not seen their like even in Cairo or Beirut. Here the East meets West, one feels, and the two mingle. Flowing robes may be made of nylon. Ultra-modern automobiles are upholstered in priceless Persian antique carpeting.

Running from east to west and north to south, and still triumphantly holding its own, stretches the great collection of open-fronted shops, representing innumerable trades, which is known as the *suk*: the market which tradition says was there when King Solomon's ships called on their voyages to the land of Punt: and where the Queen of Sheba's caravans once halted, bringing the ivory of Africa to trade for the perfumes of far Asia.

This market is truly oriental – a haphazard, winding, eminently colourful avenue of old-style commerce. It may strike a Western eye as primitive in some ways. Yet you may purchase here not only the finest products of Birmingham and Detroit, but also priceless Eastern wares. I am convinced that there is almost nothing that you cannot buy, examine or order from the world's workshops through the picturesque Jeddah *Suk*.

I bought a few things, made friends with some of the multi-lingual shopkeepers, yarned with them and drank innumerable cups of tea without milk, or coffee flavoured with cardamoms.

On the Jeddah-Mecca highway, some three kilometres out of Jeddah, you will see by the side of the road a massive futuristic palace. During the day, flags of variegated hue stream from a sort of mast mounted upon the topmost turret. By night there is an incessant, restless winking of signal lights. If you have hired a car, truck, station wagon, your driver may mutter as he passes this place: 'Long live Ba-Khashab Pasha, and all his children!' almost as if it were an invocation. He will stop for a hurried conversation with a very businesslike Arab at a window in the palace wall. Coming home that night, as the twinkling lights come into sight, he will dip his headlights in salute. Day or night, Ba-Khashab Pasha's organisation is exchanging signals with his fleet of cars.

Once Ba-Khashab was a humble, ordinary man, somewhere on the Saudi coastline, trying to earn a living by hiring out camels. Today, with the enormous expansion of transportation and the demand for vehicles of every kind, the Pasha (nobody knows where he got his title, since it is not a Saudi one) has worked his way up until he can loll in luxury – if he were not such a worker. He is small, middle-aged, lithe, laughing and likeable, and when I went to see him he asked what prospects there were of getting his boy into Eton or Oxford.

His case could be multiplied more than a hundredfold, throughout almost the length and breadth of Arabia. A new class of Arabs has grown up: the contractor, large farmer, industrialist. Some of the sheikhs and older aristocracy, it is true, have also benefited by the new prosperity. But the two groups never mix, though each has a vital function in the Arabia of today. 'Go north, to the American oil-fields of Dhaharan, if you want to see action,' said Ba-Khashab. 'Those Americans certainly are workers. And why are they successful? Because they have unknowingly applied the principles of Islam, of the Prophet, who said: "I regard myself as a worker"!'

An American to whom I spoke shortly afterwards gave me his version of the question. 'John Q. Arab certainly is learning fast. He sure is a worker. The American way of life has gone right in there, deep.'

So you can take your pick. The truth probably lies somewhere in the middle. The Arab does not like to work without knowing that it will be rewarded. And it must be rewarded, if at all possible, by something really worth while. He is, in a sense, a natural capitalist. The word he uses for 'pay' is 'my right'.

When the Americans came into the Saudi field, they offered not only substantial royalties even in advance of the sinking of the first well: they supplied a clear hope that not only would the Government benefit by a percentage of all oil extracted, but that there would be employment and scope for local enterprise. So the Arabs and Americans could do business.

The Americans were – and still are – extremely sensitive about their position in Saudi Arabia. Every one of the 12,000 foreign employees of the Arabian-American Company is schooled and drilled and dinned with the principles of the Islamic faith and the subtleties of Arabian custom. No American among them would think today of venturing anywhere except where the oil company has a right to be. And even then he lives in his robes, his headcloth and rope fillets, like an Arab desert-bred.

The Americans are in on a good thing. From Dhaharan and the surrounding deserts a million barrels of petroleum are extracted *daily*. Arabian-American is sitting, as it was put to me, 'right on top of the greatest oilfield in the world.'

To have established this bridgehead in the sternly Wahabite part of Arabia must be counted as one of the major victories of Western business. It may be said to have been a hard-won victory, from the standpoint of pure capitalism: though I am not suggesting that the Americans feel that they have had to give too much. What I can say is that Aramco is an organisation in which the winning of the oil from the sands has resulted in a sharing of advantages between Arabs and Americans alike. The Americans have built the great Mosque which is the dominating feature of the Saudi oil camp. They have drilled deep water-wells in hundreds of places, to provide vital sustenance for camels and people. They have their own technical training programme for Saudis, hospitals, clinics, shops, agricultural missions, and the rest. While a large number of foreign employees are in Dhaharan, nobody suggests that any foreigner be recruited if there is a Saudi who can do the job. Local contractors have even been set up in business by the Company, and then patronised by Aramco.

While much of the enterprise which has resulted in a new prosperity for the Saudi peninsula is directly attributable to the American spirit and sheer dogged determination, yet the gigantic personality of Abdul-Aziz Ibn Saud can conclusively be said to have been the power behind almost everything that has been accomplished during the past thirty years.

In order to understand this fully, it will be necessary to make reference to the position of Arabia in a changing world.

According to Arab tradition, mankind's first home was somewhere in the Peninsula. Some point to Aden as the site of the Garden of Eden, others to Eve's reputed grave not far out of Jeddah. It is also believed that the Mecca Kaaba was first built by Adam himself, on the model of a house of worship in Paradise, where the angels endlessly circumambulated, praising their Lord.

Further, the Arabs of today claim descent from Abraham, through Ishmael who, they hold, was the son offered by the patriarch to God. Abraham rebuilt the Kaaba and sacred shrine of Arabia, in token of repentance for having cast Hagar out into the wilderness. Hence the sanctity of Hagar's Well in the Sanctuary: the Zam-Zam, believed to be the same stream which God caused to spring miraculously for Hagar's succour.

It is, of course, well known that the Arabs and Jews are both of Semftic origin, and that their languages are derived from a similar root. There is some likelihood on the face of it that in ancient times the Arabs followed the Hebrew religious dispensation.

While the Jews, however, maintained to a greater or lesser degree their monotheism, the Arabs, in the tribal wandering throughout the great deserts, lapsed into a theology which was based upon a number of gods. These took two forms: the main deities represented the Sun, Moon and planets, while the lesser ones were totems which watched over individual tribes.

The sanctity of Mecca remained in their observances, and the Sanctuary (*Haram*) became the home of over 300 idols. The rites of pilgrimage, adapted to the worship of the gods, continued uninterruptedly.

This was the period of the *Jahiliyya* ('Days of Ignorance') which existed until the seventh century of the Christian Era, when Mohammed preached a return to monotheism.

Mohammed was, as is fairly well known, a member of the most noble clan of the Arabs, the Quraish, who were shrine-keepers at the *Haram*. It was in the mountains near Mecca that the first chapters of the Koran (literally 'The Recitation') were revealed to Mohammed, as Moslems believe, by the Archangel Gabriel.

According to this mandate, Mohammed was commanded to lead the people out of ignorance, to tell them to worship one God alone, and to follow the code of morality and law, which, Islam says, has been carried out through successive prophets: 'Every Nation has had a Warner' is the dictum. Islam, which means 'submission to the will of God', is therefore not regarded as a new religion. According to the Koran it is the modern manifestation of the preaching of Moses and Jesus. Islam thus recognises the Jewish dispensation, as does Christianity, but accepts Jesus, whom the Jews do not, on the restricted basis of his being a divinely inspired *man*, and not a divine being.

All this has a definite bearing upon Arabian and world history subsequent to Mohammed's mission.

After the persecutions and trials common to all great religious teachers, Mohammed found that his preaching had eventually converted almost all Arabia. But Islam was for the whole world: this is fundamental. So it must be spread. When he died, Mohammed had just completed his exchange of letters with neighbouring rulers, calling upon them to accept Islam.

Under Mohammed's immediate successors, the Arab tribes – unified for the first time in history – poured forth from the deserts, and conquered all North Africa to the Atlantic, all the Holy Roman Empire, and what are now Turkey, Persia and Afghanistan. Under successive dynasties, Islam became the most powerful force on earth. Moslems reached the borders of France and Austria, pushed far into China, overcame all India, marched into the Russian steppes. For several hundred years the Islamic centres of learning retrieved and developed lost sciences and became the magnet for seekers after knowledge everywhere. Islam had by now become a composite civilisation, as well as a religion and social order. With the entry of the Persian, Indian and European elements, a synthesis had been produced. For 1,000 years, scientists, mystics and artists were always able to find some permissive part of the World of Islam in which to work.

Then came the destruction of the military and cultural force of the new world-state. The irruption of the pagan Mongol hordes from Central Asia literally ground the Moslems into a mire of their own blood and the ruins of their cities, farms, universities. From this blow Islam has never really recovered. True, the Mongols eventually accepted Islam, but so much had been lost that it has taken nearly eight hundred years to revive.

Saudi Arabia became subject to Ottoman Turkey. Deep in their desert strongholds, the bedouin were little affected by what went on in the world. But they nursed their heritage: the possession of the Koran, and the knowledge that it had been under Arabs and Moslems that their power had extended from Spain to China.

The Turks were driven out of Arabia by an alliance between bedouins, Hejazi Arabs and the British, in which rebellion the late T. E. Lawrence played such a part.

But the northern area, home of the Wahabites, had never really been under effective Turkish control. Even before the First World War the Saudis – the family of Ibn Saud – were working and fighting to regain control of Nejd, their former homeland.

By 1902 the twenty-year-old Abdul-Aziz ibn Saud had captured the northern fortress of Riyadh. The descendants of the Prophet who were nominal rulers of Mecca in the south, and who co-operated with the British to throw off the Turkish yoke, had to leave, and set up their own small kingdoms in Iraq and Trans-jordan. Saud made himself master of virtually all Peninsular Arabia.

The first period of his reorganisation of the country pacified the tribes under the banner of Saud the Great. Then the 'effete' south was visited with severe punishment, and all 'extravagances' were put down. Domes and minarets were levelled, for example, as being importations foreign to the simple spirit of Islam. Although a friend of the King, for example, my father was caned in the street for lighting a cigarette.

But Ibn Saud could not go any further with his big plans for the development and uplift of seven million Arabs without more money than any Arab could conceive of at that time. For nearly twenty years Saudi Arabia depended solely upon customs dues and the few million pounds that the pilgrims brought each year for their expenses.

Then, in 1933, King Abdul-Aziz arranged with American

companies to drill for oil. I was told by one veteran of those days that the geologists were convinced that somewhere here, in the wild and hostile Wahabi country, lay the world's largest deposit. But it took them five years of wildcat (random) drilling to locate it. After they did, Saudi Arabia never had to look back.

Arabia had become front-page news. In the days just before the Second World War Germans, Italians and even the Japanese fought for oil and commercial concessions. Britain and America were reported to be at loggerheads because, it was said, Britain thought that she should have had a greater interest in the oil. Ibn Saud weathered it all. During the last war he was one of the few neutral statesmen who consistently supported the Allied cause.

When Vichy held Syria in an uneasy pro-Axis grip, and Rashid Ali el-Gailani revolted in Iraq, all seemed lost to the United Nations. Ibn Saud, as I was told in Riyadh, could easily have thrown in his lot with the Germans, and would have had little to lose. Deprived of his oil, the British and American fleets and mercantile marine would have been crippled in this part of the world. The Japanese could have made liaison with the Germans via the Arabian coastline, and the Suez route between India and Europe made completely impossible. Persia would have been outflanked. Even if the Germans had won the war, the Arabs believe that such is the value of the oilfields at Dhahran and elsewhere in Nejd, they could have negotiated a peace based upon the security of the wells: for, no matter how strong the Americans may be in this area, not one drop of oil can be pumped without active Arab friendship. This co-operation could come only through the Saudi regime. But Saud had given his word.

This survey of Arabian history has only noted the highlights. Ibn Saud's own life story, for instance, is one of the world's classic accounts of one man battling against odds which, as you read it, seem almost insane.

Equally, the fact that the Saudi royal family is now almost fabulously wealthy does not mean that they have waxed rich on oil at everyone else's expense. The very contrary is the case.

Visualise the position of Saudi Arabia in 1938, when the first royalties were coming in. Here was a country just about as underprivileged as any in the world. There were no roads, almost no electric light, no aircraft, factories, industries, banking, insurance, public security, national currency, hygiene, drainage. There was one newspaper and no radio station. Education was carried on by aged and often blind clerics, teaching small boys the Koran by heart. There were no building materials available except mud and a little wood. Where would you start? There was only one way to do it: Ibn Saud bought the lot himself.

He surrounded himself with all the talent that came his way. Most of those men were still with him when I made this visit, and I had the privilege of meeting them. There was Sheikh Abdullah El-Fadhl, the financial brain: Sheikh Hafiz Wahba, the shrewd diplomat, and Egyptian; Sheikh Abdullah Sulaiman, from the North, in charge of economic affairs; and Fuad Bey Hamza, the Syrian, who carried the country through many a crisis.

Saud, in advising Rashid Ali against military action aimed at Britain, is on record as having said: ' . . . I am a staunch friend of Great Britain, inheriting this friendship from my grandfather, Faisal Ibn Turki. When a friend is under duress, then, for the sake of friendship, one does not act against him. Personally, if I had sufficient armaments I would have gone to the help of Great Britain and not acted against her. With the exception of the question of Palestine, Great Britain did nothing against Arab interests, and the present war is one of life and death. So our duty, if unable to help Britain, is to be neutral. This is the least that I can do.'

Although King Ibn Saud declared war on Germany and Japan eventually, he did not allow this to affect in the least the age-old code of Arab and Moslem hospitality. Those Arabs who had supported the Axis Powers during the Second World War and fled to him for asylum from the Allies were unconditionally granted protection . . .

When I returned to Jeddah from Riyadh after seeing the King, I was told 'off the record' of something that had taken place just before I saw His Majesty.

Someone had got the idea that I was a spy of some sort, and this rumour had reached the King's ears. Ibn Saud thundered in open court at his informant: 'This is our guest! If he is a spy, let him spy! He will not be able to combat the strength of our faith, which is the most powerful thing that we have. And if he is not a spy, as I believe he is not, then Allah will punish you with all His power, for there is no mercy for intriguers!'

But I did not know of the whispers which had preceded me to the Court, and continued my preparations to journey Meccawards, to the Shrine of the Black Stone.

*   *   *

Do you want both egg and omelette?

Proverb.

The dead depend upon the living.

Proverb.

Pilgrimage to Mecca

Pilgrimage to Mecca

ᴚᴐ

The town was full of jostling pilgrims: old and young, male and female, white, yellow and black. They thronged the old and new parts of the town, seeking provisions for the journey to Mecca, arranging transport to the Holy City, waiting for friends whom they had agreed to meet in Mecca perhaps a year and several thousand miles away.

Though quite a number of pilgrims march southwards to Mecca by the austere route through the Nejd desert, by far the majority enter Saudi Arabia through Jeddah, either by sea or by way of the new and most impressive aerodrome. The transformation which these people all undergo as soon as they reach the holy country has to be seen to be believed. There is a saying that the Pilgrimage makes a good man better; but that it may make a bad man better or worse. Whatever the truth of this may be, there is no doubt at all that a high emotion, akin to nothing which one has felt before, grips even the most Westernised of Moslems when he sets foot even on the 'secular' soil – or sand – of Jeddah.

Apart from the regular flights of Saudi-Arabian Airways and other scheduled arrivals, Jeddah airport receives an endless succession of chartered aircraft from India, Pakistan and other Arab lands, even far-off Indonesia.

The actual atmosphere of the city differs little from that of many another town of some importance in the Middle East. The same fierce sun is here, beating down upon a mixture of modern steel and concrete office buildings with those of the Turkish and Red Sea Arab type. Open-fronted cafés, money-changers, sellers of sweetmeats and cool drinks: they are all here. There is a smaller non-Moslem population than in most Arab cities, however. One part of the city contains the magnificent foreign embassies and consulates.

It is among the pilgrims themselves that the strange other-worldly feeling exists. After the first excitement of arriving at long last on Saudi soil had passed, I made the formal vow – the *niia* – which every pilgrim resolves: and felt myself in some unique way cut off from the rest of humanity. Things like the smoking habit, like worrying about what might happen from one hour to the next, or even my future plans, all seemed to dim into a petty and more than welcome insignificance.

I stopped writing my diary, found myself almost impelled by a sense of community with tens of thousands of white-robed fellows to read and recite passages from the Islamic scriptures. One felt the need for communion with a mightier, a vaster force than mankind. Although it has been said time and again that the human mind needs some sort of intermediary – whether it be a man, or a stick or stone, an idol or picture – to concentrate upon (let alone comprehend) divinity, we pilgrims to Mecca felt no such need.

We were not there to worship the Kaaba or the Black Stone. We worshipped no man, nor did we accord divine rights or a divine character to anything save one power, which we could not visualise – and did not want or expect to be able to see. Yet in us all was a feeling of contentment, and an underlying excitement that we were about to achieve something which we had all worked for, to arrive somewhere which was dear to our hearts. We were on the verge of fulfilment. That was what we expected: and that was the nature of the sensation which we all experienced when we actually reached Mecca the Holy.

I sought out as many of my fellow pilgrims as I could, of diverse origins, both social and otherwise. It would be difficult to name an ethnic group, a social class or almost any other type which was not represented. Apart from the very large numbers from India, Pakistan and Indonesia (whence come the majority of foreign pilgrims) I 'collected' Kurds, Bosnians, Hadendowas, Tajiks – and a Japanese. Some had been Jews, others were former Christians; there was an ex-communist who had struck up a great friendship with an extremely wealthy Indian business man from Kenya.

In our sandals and new white robes we explored the fascinating byways of the older part of the city, discussing theology and Islamic history, and exchanging stories from our lives. During

these discussions, while we were waiting for our transport arrangements to Mecca, I was able to observe in some detail the change
which must have come over these people since they arrived a
matter of hours or days ago from the farthest corners of the world.

From what they said about their lives I could tell that some of
them, not so long ago, had been of that glib-tongued, thoroughly
tiresome group of Middle Eastern intellectuals who know a little
about a lot of things, and have to pour it all out as soon as they are
able to get it into words: which does not take long. Now, dedicated
to perform the visit to Mecca and the stoning of the former idols
to the north, they spoke and acted with a reasonableness which I
am very sure would have surprised even their own families.

There were at least three wealthy business men: one from
Mombasa, another with textile interests in Bombay, the third a
shipowner from Dacca. Different in race and tongue, they carried
on their conversations in English. I am quite convinced that in any
commercial contact with these men, their razor-sharp minds would
have driven a bargain which no normal person could hope to match.
They had that prosperous, horn-rimmed, well-cared-for look which
is the stamp of the tycoon anywhere. Two of them had arrived in
their own aeroplanes. Yet here, in the mellow Jeddah night, as we
sat by the edge of the curving inland bay, their thoughts and
reactions were no different from those of the gentle untutored
servants whom they had brought with them, and whose tasks they
shared.

This transformation alone is to my mind one of the wonders of
the Pilgrimage. Although I must admit that I was not in a very
critical frame of mind, I was immensely impressed by their
directness and calm. I never for a moment sensed any suggestion
of hypocrisy, any reversion to those mundane matters which must
have claimed their daily attention for upwards of twenty years.

Almost as fast as they descended upon Jeddah, the pilgrims were
making for Mecca: eastwards to the Holy City. Like a foaming,
surging tidal wave, the sea of humanity moved on and on. Barefoot
and carrying packs, mounted on mules and donkeys, perched
beneath awnings rigged up on camels, the poorer and more old-
fashioned faithful marched. Motor lorries and buses, each one
packed to overflowing with pilgrims and yet more pilgrims,

glittering new American cars, monopolised the middle of the road, and threw the black, macadamised ribbon into moving, coloured relief. From the devout concourse of dedicated humanity came a roar which seemed to cleave the shimmering heat-haze with almost physical force: '*Labbayk, Allahumma: Labbayk!*' 'Here we are, O Lord, in Thy presence!'

As my car swept past the gold and green princely palaces radiating out from Jeddah's centre, the emotion of the sound and movement of that almost unbelievable multitude gripped me with increasing force.

Load after load of white-robed devotees with shaven heads roared past. There were several hundred soldiers, chanting in rhythmic unison, their incisive voices momentarily gaining power over the unco-ordinated litany of the pedestrians: '*Lab*bayk, Allah*umma, Labbayk!* Labbayk, la sharikalak: LABBAYK! Inna al-hamda, wa anniamata – la-ka w'al mulk! *La sharikalak!*'

I felt the blood rising in my head as the accented words seized my consciousness, as it were, in an hypnotic grip: 'Here we are, O Lord, in Thy presence! We are here, we are here . . . none like unto Thee . . . verily all praise . . . all power to Thee: Thou hast no partner!' The absolute indivisibility and possession of all power are, according to Islam, supreme attributes unique to Allah.

As the trucks swept past I noticed upon their sides the sword and date tree – emblem of Saudi Arabia. Under this is the motto, in cursive Arabic letters: 'No God but Allah: (and) Mohammed (is) the Messenger of Allah.'

In sluggish contrast to the intense movement along the motorway comes the unending white flow of pedestrian worshippers, men and women, children and nurses, guides and servants. Why do they walk? Many are poor; most, however, march this final fifty miles Meccawards either to fulfil a vow, or because they feel that greater humility and piety attach to entering the Holy City afoot as Mohammed did, nearly fourteen hundred years ago. Although a conqueror, he walked thus with the Four Companions to Abraham's shrine, there to demolish the three hundred and more idols, and to establish the worship of one God alone among the people of this land.

Stretching far away to each horizon beyond the road for most of this bleak and punishing journey nothing may be sighted beyond rippling dunes of the finest, brownish sand. Here and there a bedouin woman brings her camel to a well.

Featureless is the only word to describe the plain across which we were moving. Nothing stood out from the desert to remind us of the centuries since Arabia produced a man who was to become the inspirer of hundreds of millions. We might have been projected back into the very days of the Mission.

As my faculties seemed suddenly to sharpen, I became aware of the astonishing variety in physiognomy among the surging throng. Uniform in their unstitched *Ahram* sheet, the men with one shoulder bare, there seemed to be almost no two people who resembled one another. Blond, blue-eyed chunky Syrians and Anatolian peasant types marched alongside Pathan hill-men with hooked noses and long curly black hair. Sudanese tribesmen, with finely chiselled features and cheek-marks denoting their origin, strode beside podgy, round-faced Indians – obviously far more used to sedentary activities. A Javanese under five feet tall was dwarfed by a thin, rangy woman with copper-coloured hair who was telling a ninety-nine-bead rosary of pale amber. All indications of rank or distinction, manifestation of arrogance or self-seeking, every trace of petty individuality, had vanished.

This was a collection of people such as even Hollywood could surely not hope to muster. Devoutly anxious as they undoubtedly were to reach Mecca, they were neither a rabble, nor a mere chance collection of travelling companions. This much was evident from their behaviour. If one faltered, his fellows would stop and give him a helping hand. There was no wild panic when a truck overturned, and strewed its hundred occupants over the patiently plodding foot passengers. Those who immediately surrounded the vehicle stopped and picked up the bruised ones. Nobody seemed seriously hurt. Those who came behind merely made a short detour, without crowding around to see the sight. The calm would, under any other circumstances, or anywhere else, have seemed unnatural. Here I did not give it more than a passing thought.

This road is one of absolutely first-class quality, and is kept clear of sand by the incessant motor traffic: for there are no railways in southern Saudi Arabia, though the old line from the north (which was wrecked by T. E. Lawrence's Arabs) is now being surveyed with a view to putting it into commission again.

On we went, past the interminable column of humanity, as the road climbed sharply into the iron-stained foothills beyond which the Holy City lies. This precipitous part was literally hewn from the rocks by bulldozers, which are still working on the road in some places.

Through these narrow, twisting, man-made defiles climbs the car, while something like a brief gust of delicious wind seems to move swiftly past us. Suddenly, around a bend, looms a sign, inscribed in Arabic and English:

STOP

RESTRICTED AREA. MOSLEMS ONLY

PERMITTED BEYOND THIS POINT

Saudi guards, some carrying the cane switches characteristic of Nejd, others hugging automatic weapons, come forward to inspect our credentials. Small, wiry men, their martial bearing is well set off by the khaki uniform and green Arab head-dress.

Arranging transport, guides and a hundred and one other facilities for up to a million pilgrims is a herculean task which the Pilgrimage Administration carries out without any hitch whatever. Matters of identity, documentation and quarantine are so well attended to that I felt enormous relief that I was not trying to get past this and other posts under false pretences. It has been said that non-Moslems have penetrated into Mecca undetected. Before believing it, I should have to interview such a person personally. It is not difficult to get fairly full details about the Pilgrimage, and then to write it as one's own experience. But I doubt whether anyone other than a Moslem has actually performed the pilgrimage since Burton. While, I say, it is just possible that an imposter may have done it, I am quite sure that the difficulties today are immensely greater than they were during the time of Turkish suzerainty. Saudi Arabia has all the modern methods of detection and control at her disposal: and she uses them.

This is not to say that 'a surprisingly large number' have not tried, as one police official told me . . .

After this point, fourteen miles from the city, the ruins of abandoned Turkish forts seem to brood in the baking desert silence. These strongpoints were raised by the Ottomans in an attempt to combat the brigand menace: but it took Ibn Saud's rough and ready justice to stamp out banditry in the Hejaz. Until the Napoleon of Arabia took over control, robber bands used to swoop down on pilgrim caravans, looting and killing. The performing of the *haj* used to be considered such a dangerous undertaking that pilgrims, before setting out for Arabia, made their wills and said a final goodbye to their families. As, however, pilgrimage is one of the five essential Pillars of Islam, its performance is obligatory on all believers. The other four Pillars are prayer, fasting during the daytime in the month of Ramadan, testimony to the unity of God and the prophethood of Mohammed, and the giving of alms.

Inside the Forbidden Zone, where no life – even of an animal – may be taken, we halted, to say thanksgiving prayers.

Near the spot where yet another of the Turkish forts crumbles into unregretted ruin, the King had erected a shelter and well for the dusty faithful. This one was built by the hands of Ibn Saud himself; while others are now placed at regular intervals along the road.

We passed on. It could not be far now. There was a tenseness visible in every face as we passed group after group of trudging figures, telling their rosaries or reciting passages from the Koran, which many know by heart in its entirety.

Suddenly, as we sped through the multicoloured yet austere-looking igneous rocks, the dazzlingly white panorama of Mecca swept into view, spread out below, surrounded by its seven hills. The car lost speed as from the driver's lips came yet again that glad, involuntary exclamation, echoed by every pilgrim: 'We are here, O Lord!'

So this was Mecca. Built in a hollow, surrounded by frowning crags, the many-storied houses have from a distance a strangely modern look. Yet the entire impression of the white stone city against the furrowed darkness of the crags, when seen, at any rate by a pilgrim, has something of an intoxicating quality.

I distinctly remember looking at the houses, the wide streets, the carved wooden shutters, and thinking: 'Here I am. No matter what happens, I have seen Mecca. I have reached Mecca. This is Mecca, the Holy . . . '

Had I been on foot, I am sure that I would have run forward, thrown myself on the sand, made some sort of demonstration of joy. The driver had stopped the car, and was reciting the first chapter of the Koran: '*The Opening*'.

I looked back to see the effect that Mecca was having on the other pilgrims when they first glimpsed it. It may have been because of weariness, or it may have been some other reason; but the inevitable reaction to the sight of Mecca was that the pilgrim stopped dead; stood stock-still. At first there was a look almost of unbelief on every face. Then in rising crescendo came the cry: 'There is no God but Allah, Mohammed is the Prophet of Allah!'

It echoed and re-echoed through the gathering darkness: not a chant, not a song – both are forbidden by Islam's austere interdiction against show in religion. It was more like a cry of wonder, of hope, of fulfilment . . . LA ILLAHA ILLA ALLAH: MOHAMMED AR RASUL ALLAH . . .

This is the *Tauhid*, the Confession of Faith: the first Pillar of Islam. This is the phrase which should be the first sound heard by every new-born Moslem babe; the sentence which identifies one Moslem to another, the 'contract' whose repetition establishes the moment of conversion of a person to the faith. It is part of the Call to Prayer throughout the World of Islam, and a part of every private or congregational prayer. It is the motto of the House of Saud, the war-cry of the Riff, the Turks, the Arabs, the Afghans. It is also one of the phrases which is used on almost every occasion, from a wedding to a birth, to death. Every Moslem is supposed to die with no other words on his lips . . .

The orderly mass of humanity was flooding past our stationary car now, and the driver let in the clutch, and we were off on the very last lap of a journey which had begun for all of us, in a religious sense, on the day upon which we were born.

Abundant water, drilled with the aid of modern apparatus has made a considerable difference to the appearance of the city.

Two decades before there had been only one solitary piece of vegetation in Mecca. This was 'The Tree', and people were once taken to see this wonder. Today there are gardens and palm-groves everywhere. Water is usually taken for granted by Westerners and by those of us who come from greener lands. Think what a priceless boon it is in the arid East. No wonder that, realising its value, the desert Arab may throw a few drops of the precious fluid on the sand before he slakes his thirst, murmuring, 'Let the ground drink – it is more important than I!'

It is still only one Moslem in a thousand who can manage to reach Mecca in any one year; and less than one in ten (on an average) who can get there during his lifetime, even though the pilgrimage and the visit to the House of Allah is an obligation binding upon all.

After a final check of our *bona fides* we were allowed to enter the sacred city. Everywhere there were signs of modern progress: building seemed almost to be the principal industry. The available space is becoming so limited that new villas are now being constructed higher and higher up the surrounding cliffs, which in some places actually jut into the streets in the form of rugged outcrops.

Right in the heart of the city stands the central shrine of Islam: the Great Mosque and the Sanctuary of the Kaaba. Surrounded by massive walls, the place is guarded by fierce, vigilant Wahabi warriors. A vast arena is flanked by towering minarets from which the call to prayer is made, nowadays relayed to very corner of the sacred enclosure by amplifiers. No fewer than nineteen arched gateways, richly embellished with coloured geometrical designs, pierce the walls of the *Haram* – the Sanctuary. All around the many hundreds of yards of encircling rampart run quotations from the Koran, executed in flawless calligraphy. Photography, or the making of pictures of any kind, is absolutely forbidden by Wahabi law in this hallowed area.

Once inside, through one of those gates, the worshipper removes his shoes and walks, clad only in his single cotton sheet, towards the towering black-draped Kaaba: the cube, which stands in the centre of the Sanctuary. The sanctified area itself is a vast, unroofed rectangle, surrounded on its inner sides by arched colonnades, resembling cloisters. Wide paths of white marble radiate from the Kaaba to the various gates.

Although there is no priesthood in Islam, the enormous number of foreign pilgrims who visit here without a knowledge of the customary prayers and duties have necessitated the institution of secular guides – known as *Mutawwifin*. This means 'Those who enable one to turn.' Many of these are voluntary workers, and all of them are accomplished linguists. There are said to be a thousand such guides, who conduct the pilgrims in national parties through the ceremonies. Many are well-to-do merchants of a pious bent of mind.

I arrived in Mecca at night, and would have to wait until morning to see the Afghan *Mutawwif*, who was to be my guide.

Before starting the actual pilgrimage rite at the Kaaba, however, I decided to visit the Kaaba sanctuary.

I walked through the brilliantly lighted covered market which runs along one outside wall of the Kaaba enclosure, to the gate where the booksellers' shops are located. As I approached the gateway the rising murmur of thousands of voices repeating their prayers faded from my consciousness as I glimpsed, away beyond a line of mighty pillars, the black-draped granite cube, thrown into brilliant relief against its marble surround.

Electric lighting has replaced the ancient oil-lamps of the *Haram*. Even in their harsh brilliance the immense rectangle retained that magical quality of mystery and other-worldly fascination which has been so often described by pilgrims.

I paused, wonderstruck, my senses almost reeling, certainly deeply affected. A group of newly arrived pilgrims, led by their *Mutawwif*, passed me and made their way slowly along the marble pathway towards the cube. Soon they were merged with the endlessly circumambulating figures already making their anti-clockwise circuit of the holiest place of Islam.

I walked towards this *Qibla* – the point towards which every Moslem daily turns five times in his prayers. As I was not yet sufficiently coached in the observances to join the actual ceremonies, I took up a reverent position some ten yards from the cube, to say the customary two prayers of thanksgiving.

Such is the breathtaking extent of the Sanctuary that this, the goal of every pilgrim heart, seemed the least crowded place in Holy Mecca. Away over to the right some two hundred African pilgrims were making their obeisances towards the Kaaba: yet they seemed to occupy an infinitesimal part of the arena.

Near the Kaaba stands the 'Place of Abraham', where the patriarch is reputed to have stood to say his prayers. Formerly the Four Traditionist Schools of Islam each had its own praying-place, behind which the Hanafi, Hambali, Maliki or Shafai followers – as the case might be – ranged themselves. Since the puritanical Wahabis took over Mecca, these distinctions have been abolished, though the erection (rather like small archways) still stand.

A few yards farther on is the Zam-Zam: the holy well which is believed to have originated with the spring which miraculously appeared to quench the thirst of Hagar and her child in the wilderness.* All pilgrims drink this water. Some steep a corner of their *Ahram* robe in it, for eventual use as a shroud. Day and night these places, like the gates, are patrolled by Saudi guards with canes, alert for any infraction of customary decorum.

There was no sign of the teeming pigeons which crowd the Sanctuary during daytime. One odd thing about them is that they never defile the Kaaba's covering, even though a movement among the pilgrims often causes them to wheel overhead. Neither, I was later to observe time and again, do they alight on the cube itself, though the pathways, sand, well-shelter and awnings are all covered from time to time with perching and strutting birds. These peculiarities have been noted for centuries. I was as unable as my predecessors here to find a cause for this unusual behaviour of the birds.

As soon as one party of pilgrims moved away from the Kaaba, another took its place. Day and night throughout the years, the faithful are always traversing this circuit, trudging round and round the Kaaba, making special supplications, intoning the appropriate prayers, kissing the Black Stone which is set in the lower south-east corner.

Many – if not all – of the residents of the city come here at some time during each day to perform this *Tawaf* ceremony.

Embedded in a silver setting in the Kaaba's actual granite matrix is the famous Black Stone. Its history is interesting, but generally much misunderstood by others than Moslems. Even

* Genesis xxi, 19.

today, learned Western orientalists confuse the Kaaba with the Stone.

The Stone is kissed by every worshipper after the seventh circuit of the cube. Each time he passes it, the pilgrim raises his hands, palms outwards, towards it. This attention is paid to the Stone not as an act of faith or worship, but merely because it is the only surviving relic which was touched by the prophet Mohammed, and because it was reputedly cast down from Heaven as a sign for Adam. It is said to be of meteoric origin, but I am completely convinced otherwise.

In the first place, it is not black, as I was able to see later in the daylight, but rather more of the colour and appearance of dark amber. I tapped the surface, which is distinctly not stone nor metallic. I would say that it is composed of an entirely unfamiliar substance which I would recognise again, but which I cannot describe by analogy. It seems to have perceptible characteristics which defy definition, but which make a characteristic impression on the eye and hands. One would recognise this substance if it were ever again encountered.

The heavy embroidered *Kiswa* (covering of the Kaaba) is slit at the Black Stone corner, to give access to the spot. The silver setting itself is extremely unusual in workmanship, and is shaped like an inverted bowl with a large circular hole into which one has to put one's head to kiss the Stone. In the centre is a hollow several inches deep, worn into the Stone by the kisses of millions of pilgrims.

There is a a story dating back to the time of Mohammed which is supposed to record one of his first indications of wisdom. When he was a small boy there was a dispute among the four most important clans of Mecca as to which should have the honour of nominating a chief to replace the Stone in the place from which it had been removed during repairs to the Kaaba. Tempers ran high, and eventually – in accordance with the then invariable custom of consulting omens – it was agreed that the first person to pass into the Sanctuary from outside would be allowed to judge.

As it happened it was the young Mohammed. When the dispute was referred to him, it was expected that he would favour the candidate of his own tribe, the Quraish. Instead, he advised that one chief from each tribe should take a corner of a heavy cloth in which the stone was to be laid, so that they could share the task equally. Mohammed himself lifted the Stone into the cloth, to prevent any complications as to the right of performing this task.

This story is one of those which show that the importance of the Stone goes back before Mohammed's time. But the Stone could not have been one of the three hundred idols which Mohammed later destroyed, as he would not have been allowed to permit one to survive: he himself banned anything which smacked of idolatry, and his contemporaries in the early days of Islam when idol-breaking was in vogue are on record as being of the type that would have bitterly contested any weakening from uncompromising and literal iconoclasm.

The pilgrimage to Mecca was an established part of Arab religious duty long before Mohammed. The etymology of the city's name is traceable to an ancient word for 'holy', and it seems probable that this place was indeed intimately connected with fundamental happenings in Semitic religion in times of which we have no recorded history in the modern sense.

Mohammed did not claim to be the founder of a new religion. According to Moslem belief, he merely restored the severe monotheism which was revealed to mankind through a series of prophets, of whom Jesus was one of the most important. This explains, to Moslems, why certain observances from pre-Islamic times were retained: and the same explanation is implied in the Koran. Unsympathetic or hostile students of the religion, on the other hand, claim that Islam was developed from Judaism and Christianity with a certain amount of purely Arabian religion retained. Needless to say, neither contention is capable of proof, though you would not think so if you read most generalised accounts of Islam by outsiders.

The actual rites of the pilgrimage are thus: there is the visit to the Kaaba, and its circumambulation. Then comes a sevenfold circuit barefooted between the two points known as Safa and Marwa, said to be the tombs of Hagar and Ishmael. On a certain day the entire pilgrimage sets out for a place called Mina, a few miles from Mecca, there to cast stones at three pillars which represent devils. Prayers are said on Mount Arafat, and an animal is sacrificed in commemoration of Abraham's offering. The pilgrim's head is then shaved, and there is a three-day festival of dedication to a new and purer life. Anyone who completes these observances is entitled to the style of *Haji*, and generally finds that he is revered in his native community. In some countries, those who have made the pilgrimage wear a green turban or other indication of this distinction.

Back through the crowded streets I went to my hotel, 'The Hotel of Ease and Comfort', where apartments had been prepared for official guests. Built in what seemed closest to the Moorish style, its equipment and atmosphere were altogether delightful. Servants and employers ate enormous helpings of rice and meat at the same table; in fact the dining-room had the aspect of a continuous and entirely democratic feast the whole time I was there.

My room overlooked a lush palm-garden, beyond which I could see the stately height of the Minister of National Economy's residence. I spent a few minutes in meditation on the wide, trellised verandah.

In the morning the *Mutawwif* of the Afghans called early. He was to take me and several others through the Kaaba and Safa-Marwa ceremonies. Tall, grey-bearded, robed in white with a turban tied Afghan-style, he was received with great respect by the manager and other functionaries, down to the coffee-boy.

Wearing one unstitched cotton piece around the lower part of of our bodies, with a second similar sheet (the size of a large bath-towel) over one shoulder, we walked towards the Sanctuary once again, repeating after the *Mutawwif* the vow that we had made to complete the pilgrimage, and the various other prayers. I wore – like the others – a pair of sandals with the heel and instep bare. The outfit is designed to indicate decorum and humility. No other garment, no jewellery, may be worn. In pre-Islamic times the pilgrim Arabs made the Kaaba circuit stark naked.

We entered the Sanctuary through the Gate of Ali (son-in-law and a successor of Mohammed) and walked across the sunbaked arena towards the Black Stone corner of the Kaaba, where the *Tawaf* (circumambulation) commences.

One by one we stooped to kiss the Black Stone. Then, following the guide, we started the anticlockwise circuit of the cube. The first three circuits of the Kaaba are made at a run, followed by four at walking pace. The explanation for this is that Mohammed and his small band of followers, although in a state of exhaustion, ran round the Kaaba before they were eventually allowed to perform their devotions there by the hostile Quraish. In this way they tried to show their determination and stamina.

Each time we passed the Black Stone we kissed it. When the press was too great to kiss or touch the Stone, the pilgrims raised their hands, palms outwards towards it, in a gesture similar to that used when warming the hands at a fire. Subjective or otherwise, there is a sensation of tingling experienced in the hands at these moments.

Although there were a fair number of women among the pilgrim parties, men were in the majority. The women pilgrims' dress differs from that on the men, being composed of a long white dress which covers the body and arms, but with the face bare. Women are not allowed to wear veils in the Sanctuary. The veiling of women, which was to become a Moslem custom in most Islamic countries, was in fact copied from the Christian communities in Syria by the Moslems during their conquest of that country. It was, however, known in Arabia as practised by some of the highest class of women, and hence carried with it a suggestion of arrogance which is therefore forbidden during the Pilgrimage. In actual practice today, while the town women are veiled, those of the desert are not. White stockings and gloves complete the female pilgrim's costume. The hair must be covered. It is interesting to note in passing (since unveiling is such an issue with feminist movements in the modern East) that there is no clear injunction in the Koran or Traditions of Mohammed to the effect that women should be veiled. The Koranic passage cited in defence of seclusion in reality commands that decorum and modesty be observed by believing women.

Finally kissing the Stone, we moved to the 'Praying-Place of Abraham', to say another thanksgiving prayer. It is at this point that every worshipper makes his personal supplication, asking Allah for that which is closest to his heart.

Abraham is said to have stood on this spot when he was rebuilding the Kaaba (which legend holds was erected by Adam himself on the model of the Kaaba in Paradise). Then water from the Holy

Zam-Zam well was brought by small boys chosen for this honour from among the noblest families. As I swallowed the liquid from the chased metal cup I noticed that it had a slightly tart taste, but was certainly not brackish or bitter, as it has been variously described.

After this part of the ceremonies, pilgrims must wait until the eighth of the month of Dhul-Hijja until they can start out on the trek to Mina and Arafat.

The rituals in the Holy City itself are completed by the run between the two small hills of Safa and Marwa, which course follows one outside wall of the *Haram*.

We therefore then left the *Haram*, and went to the starting-point of the course. After repeating the Testimony to the Unity of God (the Tauhid) intoned by our *Mutawwif*, we joined the throng of pilgrims running between the two points. On one side lay the mighty wall of the *Haram*, and on the other were shops mainly devoted to the sale of such items as the unique black and white rosaries which are much prized as relics of the *Hajj*. You pay what you can. If you have no money, the merchant will give you one free.

This *Sayy* ceremony being over, pilgrims return to their lodgings or to the Sanctuary, to await the eighth of Dhul-Hijja and the expedition to Mina and Arafat.

The night before the march to Arafat, the Sanctuary's rectangular space presents the most impressive sight that one could ever see. Here the pilgrims, in their hundreds of thousands, assemble for a final prayer. Seen from one of the many high houses which overlook the Kaaba arena, rank upon rank of worshippers, bending and standing erect again, bowing from every side towards the Kaaba, present an exhibition of concentrated worship which is undoubtedly unparalleled elsewhere.

The same impression is again conveyed by the Farewell Visit, which takes place after the return from Arafat and the Sacrifice. During this latter ceremony, the atmosphere is charged with an electric emotion. Within a short time – perhaps a few hours, certainly not more than a day or two – the pilgrim will be on his way back to mundane affairs, back to reality, back to a life whose very existence seems to have little reality here. There is a sadness and at the same time an exultation. Both of these sensations tug at the heartstrings for long, long afterwards, perhaps for life. Certainly I feel them still.

The expedition to Arafat is the most complicated and ritualistic part of the pilgrimage. The faithful start leaving the city for the five-mile walk to Mina at dawn on the eighth of the holy month. This exodus is even more impressive than the entry into Mecca, for this time every single pilgrim is present at the same time. Their swarming numbers resemble nothing that I have ever seen or heard of before. Almost every human being from Mecca itself is there as well. Shops are shut, streets are deserted. It seems as if the very human race itself, in its entirety, is on the move. The night of the eighth to ninth of the month is spent camping out. Visualise a million people in the desert under canvas at one place. Can you? It is a sight which swamps the senses so that they seem able to perceive only the small, individual happenings against the sheer immensity of what is going on.

The following day the entire concourse moves off, another ten miles along the road, to Mount Arafat, and camps in the plain around the mountain. Somewhere among them, garbed in his pilgrim white, unguarded and very often unrecognised, is the King of Saudi Arabia, Protector of the Holy Places.

Prayers are said on the mountaintop, following the precedent established by the Prophet on his Farewell Pilgrimage, made after a premonition just before his death. Then three stone pillars (the 'devils') are stoned, in emulation of Abraham's putting the devil to flight when he tried to tempt him here, as the tradition has it.

The tenth of the month is the day of sacrifice, when every pilgrim must give an animal, in commemoration of Abraham offering his son as a sacrifice to God. This is the start of the Feast of Id El Adha, the Festival of Sacrifice, which is celebrated at the same time in every other Moslem country. The 'devils' are stoned twice, and before the sacrifice the pilgrims return to Mecca, to say a prayer in the Kaaba once more, and follow the Safa and Marwa pilgrim way. Finally, a piece of hair is cut or shaved from the right side of the head, then the entire head is shaved.

As I sat in the shaded courtyard, meditating upon these events, only the minarets of the Mosque could be seen above the towering Kaaba, with its gold-embroidered black mantle. This is the heavy damask *Kiswa*, which is embroidered with quotations from the Koran, and is an annual gift from Egypt. Each year the old covering is cut up and the pieces distributed among the more fortunate pilgrims, as highly prized relics. Water from the Holy Well, too, is supplied in rounded tins, and carried to the ends of the earth, sometimes to be sprinkled upon the pilgrim's grave.

Through the heat-haze I got a glimpse of the surrounding hills. All around me rested pilgrims from a hundred countries, some telling their beads, others offering prayers. The tough-looking Wahabi bedouin guards strode alertly up and down, on the watch for any impropriety.

From the *Haram's* administration building, with immense glass windows commanding the quadrangle, officials maintained a ceaseless vigil. I observed that the entire area of the Sanctuary was regularly swept by the field-glasses of these functionaries.

Thousands of pigeons wheeled overhead. Some traditions say that Gabriel sometimes came in the form of a pigeon, and whispered the Koran as it was being revealed in Mohammed's ear.

At one time pilgrims were frequently overcome by the terrific heat in this enclosed courtyard, for it sometimes reaches 133 degrees Fahrenheit in the shade! Recently, however, up-to-date innovations have vastly improved conditions here. Electric fans have been installed in the colonnades; huge, retractable blinds shield part of the periphery from the truly burning sun. Electricity lights the Sanctuary and provides power for the Zam-Zam's pumps, and maintenance work goes on endlessly throughout the enormous area.

When I spoke to the local people about the many improvements which the King had made towards the comfort of Mecca, they often said: 'Allah has rewarded him for it: was he not given bottomless wells of oil?'

Thoughts from Omar Khayyam

Thoughts from Omar Khayyam

TO GOD

RELIGIONISTS do not know Thy mercy as we know it.
A stranger cannot know Thee as does a friend.
Thou saidst: 'Sin, and I shall cast thee into Hell!'
Tell that to the person who does not know Thee!

I FLEW

I was a hawk. I flew from the secret world
Desiring to wing at once to heights.
But as I found none worthy of the Secret
I went back by the door through which I came.

CLOSED EYES

Men's eyes are closed, like blindfold mill-oxen,
Seeking like ants under a reversed cup . . .
You have not done what your forebears did – yet you want to
be like them. Knock on the Door . . .

MIRROR

I am a mirror and, who looks in me –
Whatever good or bad he speaks, he speaks of himself.

I AM

They say that I am a wine-worshipper – I am
They say that I am an adept – I am;
Do not look so much at my exterior
For in my interior I am, I am.

FOLLOW THE GUIDE

Read what you should read. See what you should see.
Act as you should act. Feel what you should feel.
Until you can do all these things, follow the Guide.
When you can do these things, you will not have to be told –
Follow the Guide.

*   *   *

A snake's child is precious to the snake.

Proverb.

Others sowed for me: I sow for others to come.

Proverb.

Meditations of Rumi

Meditations of Rumi

ᴛʜᴇʀᴇ is no cause for fear. It is imagination, blocking you as a
wooden bolt holds the door. Burn that bar . . .

*   *   *

Every thought has a parallel action.

Every prayer has a sound and a physical form.

The man of God is not an expert made by books.

First you were mineral, then vegetable, then man. You will be
an angel, and you will pass beyond that too.

There are a thousand forms of mind.

If the sea-water did not rise into the sky, where would the garden
get its life?

A totally wise man would cease to exist in the ordinary sense.

You make no spark by striking earth on a flint.

The worker is hidden in the workshop.

To the ignorant, a pearl seems a mere stone.

If a tree could move on foot or feather, it would not suffer the
agony of the saw nor the wounds of the blade.

What bread looks like depends upon whether you are hungry
or not.

You may seek a furnace, but it would burn you. Perhaps you
need only the weaker flame of a lamp.

Counterfeiters exist because there is such a thing as real gold.

Whoever says everything is true is a fool, whoever says all is untrue is a liar.

A great obstacle in the Path is fame.

God's mirror: the front is the heart, its back the world.

The infinite universe lies beyond this world.

They say: 'He cannot be found' . . . Something that cannot be 'found' is what I desire.

To make wine, you must ferment the grape juice.

Water does not run uphill.

You have two 'heads'. The original, which is concealed, the derivative, which is the visible one.

The moment you entered this world of form, an escape ladder was put out for you.

Wool only becomes a carpet because knowledge is available.

To boil water you need an intermediary – the vessel.

*   *   *

The answer to a fool is silence.

Proverb.

Short Stories

The Tale of Melon City

THE ruler of a certain city one day decided that he would like a triumphal arch built, so that he could ride under it with all pomp, for the desirable edification of the multitude. But when the great moment came, his crown was knocked off: the arch had been built too low.

The ruler therefore ordained, in his rightful wrath, that the chief of the builders should be hanged. Gallows were prepared, but – as he was being taken to the place of execution – the Master-Builder called out that it was all the fault of the workmen, who had done the actual construction job.

The king, with his customary sense of justice, called the workers to account. But they escaped the charge by explaining that the masons had made the bricks of the wrong size. And the masons said that they had only carried out the orders of the architect. He, in turn, reminded the king that his Majesty had, at the last moment, made some amendments of his own to the plans, changing them.

'Summon the wisest man in the country,' said the ruler, 'for this is undoubtedly a difficult problem, and we need counsel.'

The wisest man was carried in, unable to stand on his own feet, so ancient (and therefore so wise) was he. 'It is evident,' he quavered, 'that in law the actual culprit must be punished, and that is, in this case, quite evidently, none other than the arch itself.'

Applauding his decision, the King ordered that the offending arch be carried to the scaffold. But as it was being taken there, one of the Royal Councillors pointed out that this arch was something which had actually touched the august head of the monarch and must surely never be disgraced by the rope of execution.

As in the meantime, exhausted by his exertions, the venerable wise man had breathed his last, the people were unable to apply to him for an interpretation of this new observation. The doctors of Law, however, decreed that the *lower* part of the arch, which had not touched anything at all, could be hanged for the crime of the whole arch.

But when the executioner tried to put the arch into the noose, he found that the rope was too short. The rope-maker was called, but he soon explained that in his opinion it was the scaffold that was too high. He suggested that the carpenters were at fault.

'The crowd is getting impatient,' said the king, 'and we must therefore quickly find someone to hang. We can postpone the consideration of finer points like guilt until a later, more convenient, occasion.'

In a surprisingly short time, all the people in the city had been carefully measured, but only one was found to be tall enough to fit the gallows. It was the king himself. Such was the popular enthusiasm at the discovery of a man who would fit, that the king had to conform, and he was hanged.

'Thank goodness we found someone,' said the Prime Minister, 'for if we had not satisfied the appetite of the mob, they would undoubtedly have turned against the Crown.'

But there were important matters to consider, for almost at once it was realised that the king was dead. 'In conformity with custom,' announced the heralds in the streets, 'the first man who passes the city gate shall decide who is to be our next great ruler.'

The very next man to wander past the gate was an idiot. He was quite unlike the ordinary sensible citizens with whom we have become familiar, and when he was asked who should be king, immediately said: 'A melon.' This was because he always said 'A melon' to every question. In fact, he thought about nothing else, being very fond of melons.

And thus it came about that a melon was, with due ceremony, crowned.

Now that was years and years ago. Nowadays, when people ask the inhabitants of that land why their king seems to be a melon, they say: 'Because of the customary choice. His Majesty evidently desires to be a melon. Certainly we shall allow him to remain one until his further pleasure be known. He has, in our country, every right to be what he wants to be. We are content with that, so long as he does not interfere in our lives.'

Haughty and Generous

A CERTAIN rich man named Khalil was famed far and wide for his ability to maintain, at one and the same time, the two character-istics of hauteur and generosity which are held by many people to produce the ideal nature.

He had a friend called Aziz, a rich merchant, whose affairs came to grief through some disastrous commercial transaction.

Aziz called his son Ali and said to him:

'My son, go to the haughty and generous Khalil, tell him that your father has sent you, ask him to loan me a camel-load of silver, if he will be so generous, which I shall repay with profit to him when my affairs are once again in order.'

Ali set off for the house of Khalil. When he arrived there he was shown into the audience-hall, where Khalil was sitting. He was so haughty that he would hardly look upon the youth, and sat with his face averted from the company.

It was only after several hours that Ali was able to make his request.

Khalil looked at him with the utmost hauteur, and said: 'Leave my presence immediately!'

As the wretched Ali was making his way back through the courtyard of the house, he was handed the leading-rein of a long string of camels, each one loaded with as many sacks of gold and jewels and robes of honour as it could carry.

Aziz was overjoyed when Ali returned with the treasures, and after many months of trading he amassed a huge profit. He said to Ali:

'My son, here is a caravan with double the amount of wealth which Khalil so generously, albeit haughtily, lent us. Hasten and deliver it to him, with the gratitude of your father.'

Ali made his way again to Khalil's house, this time gaining admission only after waiting for several days.

When at last he was allowed to speak to Khalil, who was still sitting in the same manner, as if he had never moved, he said:

'Noble Sir, I am Ali, son of Aziz, come with my father's thanks and greetings, to return, together with a legitimate profit, the amount of money which you had in your generosity lent to a beggar without any security.'

Khalil looked at him for a long time. Then he said:

'Ali, son of Aziz, you and your father, though impressed, cannot understand the nature and extent of my chief characteristics! Get out of here, with your money and your camels and your goods! Generosity is not lending. I am not your father's banker.'

*　　*　　*

If you regret kissing me – take back your kiss.

Proverb.

May your shadow never grow less.

Proverb.

The Chests of Gold

ᑲᑲᑲᑲᑲᑲᑲᑲᑲᑲᑲᑲᑲᑲᑲᑲᑲᑲᑲᑲᑲᑲᑲᑲᑲᑲᑲᑲᑲᑲᑲ

ONCE upon a time there was a rich merchant who went away on a long journey, leaving his steward in charge of his money.

A crafty and dishonest man overheard him say to the steward:

'You are in sole charge. I have in my strong-room a hundred chests of gold. In each chest there are a hundred gold pieces. Guard them well until I return.'

The crafty man scraped up an acquaintanceship with the steward, and they often used to sit drinking coffee together.

One day the crafty man said: 'I am something of an alchemist. If I can get one gold piece, I can double it, so that it becomes two.'

At first the steward did not believe him; but after a time he was tempted to make a test, using some of his employer's money.

'You only borrow it,' said the crafty man, 'and you keep it in your own hands, here in the coffee-house. If it does not multiply, what can you lose?'

Eventually the steward agreed.

He took one gold piece from his master's hoard and put it in a cunningly-contrived box which the 'alchemist' supplied. When they opened the lid, there were two pieces inside.

Thus encouraged, and being presented with the extra piece as a gift, the steward asked the alchemist if he could repeat the process.

'Certainly,' said the crafty man, 'but there are certain rules. First you must take only one coin from each box of coins that you have, however many that may be. Bring them here.'

The steward did as he was told, and, one by one, the hundred coins became two hundred.

'Now for the next rule,' said the crafty man; 'and that is: you must not replace "doubled coins" in the same box. Get another box and put the two hundred in that. Then spend from the new box until your own hundred are finished. This will leave your master's capital untouched, and you will have gained one hundred pieces of gold.'

The steward did as he was told. He started to spend his own

share and, sure enough, he found that the 'doubled' pieces were real gold, accepted without question in the shops.

He had never had so much money in his life, and he spent a lot of it on drink and other personal indulgences, encouraged by the 'alchemist' who told him: 'As soon as that hundred is finished, tell me, and we will be able to repeat the process – but not before.'

When the time came for the merchant's return, the steward was well addicted to drink. The merchant, when he saw him, said: 'What kind of a steward are you? I suppose that you have spent my money on yourself?'

'On the contrary,' mumbled the steward, 'I have multiplied it.' The merchant ran to his hoard, but there did not seem to be anything missing, so far as he could see.

At that moment the crafty man appeared on the scene and said to the merchant: 'Give me the money that you have been keeping for me!'

'What money?' said the merchant; 'I have never seen you before in my life.'

Such an argument started that the police were called, and they carried the pair to the court of summary judgment.

'This man has my money, which he was keeping for me,' said the thief to the judge.

'How much do you say it is?' said the judge.

'Nine thousand, nine hundred and fifty gold pieces; ninety-nine to a chest, one chest with only fifty pieces in it,' said the crafty man, who had been keeping count of what the steward spent.

'That is a lie and I can prove it!' said the merchant. 'I had a hundred boxes with a hundred pieces in each, which I left with my steward. There is either that amount left, which is 10,000 gold pieces in all; or something less than that, if the steward has been robbing me. There cannot be the number that this man says.'

An order was made by the court to inspect the gold. It was found to tally exactly with the thief's story. The steward was regarded as bereft of his reason by alcoholism and could not be admitted as a witness. The court awarded the whole of the money to the crafty man, who became a popular and respected citizen.

The Lowest of the Arabs

THE Caliph Haroun el-Raschid was of the Prophet's tribe, but not being descended from him, was considered to be lower in rank than the Sayeds of the Hashimite Clan.

But he was – after all – an emperor, and when he heard that a certain Sayed was being hailed by his followers as 'Noblest of All the Arabs' he called the man before him.

'O Sayed!' said the Caliph, 'I am junior in descent to you, since you are of the blood of the Holy Prophet. But have you not heard that the Messenger formally abolished all title to nobility based upon blood?'

'In that case,' said the Sayed, 'I am still the Noblest of All the Arabs.'

'How can that be?' asked the Caliph.

'Even the lowliest of the Arabs, once brought into the presence of such a king, must consider this honour to elevate him to the rank of Noblest of the Arabs,' said the Sayed.

*　　*　　*

Now that it is gone, does it matter whether a cow ate it or not?
Proverb.

The Man, the Snake, and the Stone

ぴあ

ONE day a man who had not a care in the world was walking along a road. An unusual object to one side of him caught his eye. 'I must find out what this is,' he said to himself.

As he came up to it, he saw that it was a large, very flat stone.

'I must find out what is underneath this,' he told himself. And he lifted the stone.

No sooner had he done so than he heard a loud, hissing sound, and a huge snake came gliding out from a hole under the stone. The man dropped the stone in alarm. The snake wound itself into a coil, and said to him:

'Now I am going to kill you, for I am a venomous snake.'

'But I have released you,' said the man, 'how can you repay good with evil? Such an action would not accord with reasonable behaviour.'

'In the first place,' said the snake, 'you lifted the stone from curiosity and in ignorance of the possible consequences. How can this now suddenly become "I have released you"?'

'We must always try to return to reasonable behaviour, when we stop to think,' murmured the man.

'Return to it when you think invoking it might suit your interests,' said the snake.

'Yes,' said the man, 'I was a fool to expect reasonable behaviour from a snake.'

'From a snake, expect snake-behaviour,' said the snake. 'To a snake, snake-behaviour is what can be regarded as reasonable.'

'Now I am going to kill you,' it continued.

'Please do not kill me,' said the man, 'give me another chance. You have taught me about curiosity, reasonable behaviour and snake-behaviour. Now you would kill me before I can put this knowledge into action.'

'Very well,' said the snake, 'I shall give you another chance. I shall come along with you on your journey. We will ask the next creature whom we meet, who shall be neither a man nor a snake, to adjudicate between us.'

The man agreed, and they started on their way.

Before long they came to a flock of sheep in a field. The snake stopped, and the man cried to the sheep:

'Sheep, sheep, please save me! This snake intends to kill me. If you tell him not to do so he will spare me. Give a verdict in my favour, for I am a man, the friend of sheep.'

One of the sheep answered:

'We have been put out into this field after serving a man for many years. We have given him wool year after year, and now that we are old, tomorrow he will kill us for mutton. That is the measure of the generosity of men. Snake, kill that man!'

The snake reared up and his green eyes glittered as he said to the man: 'This is how your friends see you. I shudder to think what your enemies are like!'

'Give me one more chance,' cried the man in desperation. 'Please let us find someone else to give an opinion, so that my life may be spared.'

'I do not want to be as unreasonable as you think I am,' said the snake, 'and I will therefore continue in accordance with your pattern, and not with mine. Let us ask the next individual whom we may meet – being neither a man nor a snake – what your fate is to be.'

The man thanked the snake, and they continued on their journey.

Presently they came upon a lone horse, standing hobbled in a field. The snake addressed him:

'Horse, horse, why are you hobbled like that?'

The horse said:

'For many years I served a man. He gave me food, for which I had not asked, and he taught me to serve him. He said that this was in exchange for the food and stable. Now that I am too infirm to work, he has decided to sell me soon for horse-meat. I am hobbled because the man thinks that if I roam over this field I will eat too much of his grass.'

'Do not make this horse my judge, for God's sake!' exclaimed the man.

'According to our compact,' said the snake inexorably, 'this man and I have agreed to have our case judged by you.'

He outlined the matter, and the horse said:

'Snake, it is beyond my capabilities and not in my nature to kill a man. But I feel that you, as a snake, have no alternative but to do so if a man is in your power.'

'If you will give me just one more chance,' begged the man, 'I am sure that something will come to my aid. I have been unlucky on this journey so far, and have only come across creatures who have a grudge. Let us therefore choose some animal which has no such knowledge and hence no generalised animosity towards my kind.'

'People do not know snakes,' said the snake, 'and yet they seem to have a generalised animosity towards them. But I am willing to give you just one more chance.'

They continued their journey.

Soon they saw a fox, lying asleep under a bush beside the road. The man woke the fox gently, and said:

'Fear nothing, brother fox. My case is such-and-such, and my future depends upon your decision. The snake will give me no further chance, so only your generosity or altruism can help me.'

The fox thought for a moment, and then he said:

'I am not sure that only generosity or altruism can operate here. But I will engage myself in this matter. In order to come to a decision I must rely upon something more than hearsay. We must demonstrate as well. Come, let us return to the beginning of your journey, and examine the facts on the spot.'

They returned to where the first encounter had taken place.

'Now we will reconstruct the situation,' said the fox; 'snake, be so good as to take your place once more, in your hole under that flat stone.'

The man lifted the stone, and the snake coiled itself up in the hollow beneath it. The man let the stone fall.

The snake was now trapped again, and the fox, turning to the man, said: 'We have returned to the beginning. The snake cannot get out unless you release him. He leaves our story at this point.'

'Thank you, thank you,' said the man, his eyes full of tears.

'Thanks are not enough, brother,' said the fox; 'In addition to generosity and altruism there is the matter of my payment.'

'How can you enforce payment?' asked the man.

THE MAN, THE SNAKE, AND THE STONE

'Anyone who can solve the problem which I have just concluded,' said the fox, 'is well able to take care of such a detail as that. I again invite you to recompense me, from fear if not from any sense of justice. Shall we call it, in your words, being "reasonable"?'

The man said:

'Very well, come to my house and I will give you a chicken.'

They went to the man's house. The man went into his chicken-coop, and came back in a moment with a bulging sack. The fox seized it and was about to open it when the man said:

'Friend fox, do not open the sack here. I have human neighbours and they should not know that I am co-operating with a fox. They might kill you, as well as censuring me.'

'That is a reasonable thought,' said the fox; 'what do you suggest I do?'

'Do you see that clump of trees yonder?' said the man, pointing. 'Yes,' said the fox.

'You run with the sack into that cover, and you will be able to enjoy your meal unmolested.'

The fox ran off.

As soon as he reached the trees a party of hunters, whom the man knew would be there, caught him. He leaves our story here.

And the man? His future is yet to come.

*　　*　　*

A drum is not beaten under a coverlet.

Proverb.

The Value of Kingdoms

KING Bayazid was brought from the battlefield and taken before the victorious Tamerlane the Conqueror, Timur the Lame.

As soon as he saw that Bayazid had only one eye, Timur started to laugh uncontrollably.

Bayazid addressed him:

'You may laugh at my defeat, but you would do better to reflect that you might have been here, in my place. God it is who presides over the destiny of thrones. Man should not laugh at the manifestations of His Will.'

Timur, when he recovered himself, answered:

'It is that very same thought which *does* make me laugh. God indeed, presides over thrones: but they are of such little importance to him, it seems, that he hands over the kingdom of a one-eyed man to a one-legged one.'

* * *

A cart is the word for something which moves.

Proverb.

The Magic Horse

THIS tale is of great importance because it belongs to an instructional corpus of mystical materials with inner content but – beyond entertainment value – without immediate external significance.

The teaching-story was brought to perfection as a communication instrument many thousands of years ago. The fact that it has not developed greatly since then has caused people obsessed by some theories of our current civilisations to regard it as the product of a less enlightened time. They feel that it must surely be little more than a literary curiosity, something fit for children, the projection, perhaps, of infantile desires, a means of enacting a wish-fulfilment.

Hardly anything could be further from the truth of such pseudo-philosophical, certainly unscientific, imaginings. Many teaching-stories *are* entertaining to children and to naive peasants. Many of them in the forms in which they are viewed by conditioned theorists have been so processed by unregenerate amateurs that their effective content is distorted. Some apply only to certain communities, depending upon special circumstances for their correct unfolding : circumstances whose absence effectively prevents the action of which they are capable.

So little is known to the academics, the scholars and the intellectuals of this world about these materials, that there is no word in modern languages which has been set aside to describe them.

But the teaching-story exists, nevertheless. It is a part of the most priceless heritage of mankind.

Real teaching-stories are not to be confused with parables; which are adequate enough in their intention, but still on a lower level of material, generally confined to the inculcation of moralistic principles, not the assistance of interior movement of the human mind. What we often take on the lower level of parable, however, can sometimes be seen by real specialists as teaching-stories; especially when experienced under the correct conditions.

CARAVAN OF DREAMS

Unlike the parable, the meaning of the teaching-story cannot be unravelled by ordinary intellectual methods alone. Its action is direct and certain, upon the innermost part of the human being, an action incapable of manifestation by means of the emotional or intellectual apparatus.

The closest that we can come to describing its effect is to say that it connects with a part of the individual which cannot be reached by any other convention, and that it establishes in him or in her a means of communication with a non-verbalised truth beyond the customary limitations of our familiar dimensions.

Some teaching-stories cannot now be reclaimed because of the literary and traditionalistic, even ideological, processing to which they have been subjected. The worst of such processes is the historicising one, where a community comes to believe that one of their former teaching-stories represents literal historical truth.

This tale is given here in a form which is innocent of this and other kinds of maltreatment.

*   *   *   *

Once upon a time – not so very long ago – there was a realm in which the people were exceedingly prosperous. All kinds of discoveries had been made by them, in the growing of plants, in harvesting and preserving fruits, and in making objects for sale to other countries: and in many other practical arts.

Their ruler was unusually enlightened, and he encouraged new discoveries and activities, because he knew of their advantages for his people.

He had a son named Hoshyar, who was expert in using strange contrivances, and another – called Tambal – a dreamer, who seemed interested only in things which were of little value in the eyes of the citizens.

From time to time the king, who was named King Mumkin, circulated announcements to this effect:

'Let all those who have notable devices and useful
   artefacts present them to the palace for examination, so
   that they may be appropriately rewarded.'

Now there were two men of that country – an ironsmith and a woodworker – who were great rivals in most things, and each delighted in making strange contraptions. When they heard this announcement one day, they agreed to compete for an award, so that their relative merits could be decided once and for all, by their sovereign, and publicly recognised.

Accordingly, the smith worked day and night on a mighty engine, employing a multitude of talented specialists, and surrounding his workshop with high walls so that his devices and methods should not become known.

At the same time the woodworker took his simple tools and went into a forest where, after long and solitary reflection, he prepared his own masterpiece.

News of the rivalry spread, and people thought that the smith must easily win, for his cunning works had been seen before, and while the woodworker's products were generally admired, they were only of occasional and undramatic use.

When both were ready, the king received them in open court.

The smith produced an immense metallic fish which could, he said, swim in and under the water. It could carry large quantities of freight over the land. It could burrow into the earth; and it could even fly slowly through the air. At first the court found it hard to believe that there could be such a wonder made by man: but when the smith and his assistants demonstrated it, the king was overjoyed and declared the smith among the most honoured in the land, with a special rank and the title of 'Benefactor of the Community'.

Prince Hoshyar was placed in charge of the making of the wondrous fishes, and the services of this new device became available to all mankind.

Everyone blessed the smith and Hoshyar, as well as the benign and sagacious monarch whom they loved so much.

In the excitement, the self-effacing carpenter had been all but forgotten. Then, one day, someone said: 'But what about the contest? Where is the entry of the woodworker? We all know him to be an ingenious man. Perhaps he has produced something useful.'

'How could anything possibly be as useful as the Wondrous Fishes?' asked Hoshyar. And many of the courtiers and the people agreed with him.

But one day the king was bored. He had become accustomed to the novelty of the fishes and the reports of the wonders which they so regularly performed. He said: 'Call the woodcarver, for I would now like to see what he has made.'

The simple woodcarver came into the throne-room, carrying a parcel, wrapped in coarse cloth. As the whole court craned forward to see what he had, he took off the covering to reveal – a wooden horse. It was well enough carved, and it had some intricate patterning chiselled into it, as well as being decorated with coloured paints but it was only . . . 'A mere plaything!' snapped the king.

'But, Father,' said Prince Tambal, 'let us ask the man what it is for . . .'

'Very well,' said the king, 'what is it for?'

'Your majesty,' stammered the woodcarver, 'it is a magic horse. It does not look impressive, but it has, as it were, its own inner senses. Unlike the fish, which has to be directed, this horse can interpret the desires of the rider, and carry him wherever he needs to go.'

'Such a stupidity is fit only for Tambal,' murmured the chief minister at the king's elbow; 'it cannot have any real advantage when measured against the wondrous fish.'

The woodcarver was preparing sadly to depart when Tambal said: 'Father, let me have the wooden horse.'

'All right,' said the king, 'give it to him. Take the woodcarver away and tie him on a tree somewhere, so that he will realise that our time is valuable. Let him contemplate the prosperity which the wondrous fish has brought us, and perhaps after some time we shall let him go free, to practise whatever he may have learned of real industriousness, through true reflection.'

The woodcarver was taken away, and Prince Tambal left the court carrying the magic horse.

Tambal took the horse to his quarters, where he discovered that it had several knobs, cunningly concealed in the carved designs. When these were turned in a certain manner, the horse – together with anyone mounted on it – rose into the air and sped to whatever place was in the mind of the person who moved the knobs.

THE MAGIC HORSE

In this way, day after day, Tambal flew to places which he had never visited before. By this process he came to know a great many things. He took the horse everywhere with him.

One day he met Hoshyar, who said to him: 'Carrying a wooden horse is a fit occupation for such as you. As for me, I am working for the good of all, towards my heart's desire!'

Tambal thought: 'I wish I knew what was the good of all. And I wish I could know what my heart's desire is.'

When he was next in his room, he sat upon the horse and thought: 'I would like to find my heart's desire.' At the same time he moved some of the knobs on the horse's neck.

Swifter than light the horse rose into the air and carried the prince a thousand days' ordinary journey away, to a far kingdom, ruled by a magician-king.

The king, whose name was Kahana, had a beautiful daughter called Precious Pearl, Durri-Karima. In order to protect her, he had imprisoned her in a circling palace, which wheeled in the sky, higher than any mortal could reach. As he was approaching the magic land, Tambal saw the glittering palace in the heavens, and alighted there.

The princess and the young horseman met and fell in love.

'My father will never allow us to marry,' she said; 'for he had ordained that I become the wife of the son of another magician-king who lives across the cold desert to the east of our homeland. He has vowed that when I am old enough I shall cement the unity of the two kingdoms by this marriage. His will has never been successfully opposed.'

'I will go and try to reason with him,' answered Tambal, as he mounted the magic horse again.

But when he descended into the magic land there were so many new and exciting things to see that the did not hurry to the palace. When at length he approached it, the drum at the gate, indicating the absence of the king, was already beating.

'He has gone to visit his daughter in the Whirling Palace,' said a passer-by when Tambal asked him when the king might be back; 'and he usually spends several hours at a time with her.'

Tambal went to a quiet place where he willed the horse to carry him to the king's own apartment. 'I will approach him at his own home,' he thought to himself, 'for if I go to the Whirling Palace without his permission he may be angry.'

He hid behind some curtains in the palace when he got there, and lay down to sleep.

Meanwhile, unable to keep her secret, the princess Precious Pearl had confessed to her father that she had been visited by a man on a flying horse, and that he wanted to marry her. Kahana was furious.

He placed sentries around the Whirling Palace, and returned to his own apartment to think things over. As soon as he entered his bedchamber, one of the tongueless magic servants guarding it pointed to the wooden horse lying in a corner. 'Aha!' exclaimed the magician-king. 'Now I have him. Let us look at this horse and see what manner of thing it may be.'

As he and his servants were examining the horse, the prince managed to slip away and conceal himself in another part of the palace.

After twisting the knobs, tapping the horse and generally trying to understand how it worked, the king was baffled. 'Take that thing away. It has no virtue now, even if it ever had any,' he said. 'It is just a trifle, fit for children.'

The horse was put into a store-cupboard.

Now King Kahana thought that he should make arrangements for his daughter's wedding without delay, in case the fugitive might have other powers or devices with which to try to win her. So he called her to his own palace and sent a message to the other magician-king, asking that the prince who was to marry her be sent to claim his bride.

Meanwhile Prince Tambal, escaping from the palace by night when some guards were asleep, decided that he must try to return to his own country. His quest for his heart's desire now seemed almost hopeless. 'If it takes me the rest of my life,' he said to himself, 'I shall come back here, bringing troops to take this kingdom by force. I can only do that by convincing my father that I must have his help to attain my heart's desire.'

So saying, he set off. Never was a man worse equipped for such a journey. An alien, travelling on foot, without any kind of provisions, facing pitiless heat and freezing nights interspersed with sandstorms, he soon became hopelessly lost in the desert.

Now, in his delirium, Tambal started to blame himself, his father, the magician-king, the woodcarver, even the princess and the magic horse itself. Sometimes he thought he saw water ahead of him, sometimes fair cities, sometimes he felt elated, sometimes incomparably sad. Sometimes he even thought that he had companions in his difficulties, but when he shook himself he saw that he was quite alone.

He seemed to have been travelling for an eternity. Suddenly, when he had given up and started again several times, he saw something directly in front of him. It looked like a mirage: a garden, full of delicious fruits, sparkling and almost, as it were, beckoning him towards them.

Tambal did not at first take much notice of this, but soon, as he walked, he saw that he was indeed passing through such a garden. He gathered some of the fruits and tasted them cautiously. They were delicious. They took away his fear as well as his hunger and thirst. When he was full, he lay down in the shade of a huge and welcoming tree and fell asleep.

When he woke up he felt well enough, but something seemed to be wrong. Running to a nearby pool, he looked at his reflection in the water. Staring up at him was a horrible apparition. It had a long beard, curved horns, ears a foot long. He looked down at his hands. They were covered with fur.

Was it a nightmare? He tried to wake himself, but all the pinching and pummelling had no effect. Now, almost bereft of his senses, beside himself with fear and horror, thrown into transports of screaming, racked with sobs, he threw himself on the ground. 'Whether I live or die,' he thought, 'these accursed fruits have finally ruined me. Even with the greatest army of all time, conquest will not help me. Nobody would marry me now, much less the Princess Precious Pearl. And I cannot imagine the beast who would not be terrified at the sight of me – let alone my heart's desire!' And he lost consciousness.

When he woke again, it was dark and a light was approaching through the groves of silent trees. Fear and hope struggled in him. As it came closer he saw that the light was from a lamp enclosed in a brilliant starlike shape, and it was carried by a bearded man, who walked in the pool of brightness which it cast around.

The man saw him. 'My son,' he said, 'you have been affected by the influences of this place. If I had not come past, you would have remained just another beast of this enchanted grove, for there are many more like you. But I can help you.'

Tambal wondered whether this man was a fiend in disguise, perhaps the very owner of the evil trees. But, as his sense came back he realised that he had nothing to lose.

'Help me, father,' he said to the sage.

'If you really want your heart's desire,' said the other man, 'you have only to fix this desire firmly in your mind, not thinking of the fruit. You then have to take up some of the dried fruits, not the fresh, delicious ones, lying at the foot of all these trees, and eat them. Then follow your destiny.'

So saying, he walked away.

While the sage's light disappeared into the darkness, Tambal saw that the moon was rising, and in its rays he could see that there were indeed piles of dried fruits under every tree.

He gathered some and ate them as quickly as he could.

Slowly, as he watched, the fur disappeared from his hands and arms. The horns first shrank, then vanished. The beard fell away. He was himself again. By now it was first light, and in the dawn he heard the tinkling of camel bells. A procession was coming through the enchanted forest.

It was undoubtedly the cavalcade of some important personage, on a long journey. As Tambal stood there, two outriders detached themselves from the glittering escort and galloped up to him.

'In the name of the Prince, our lord, we demand some of your fruit. His celestial Highness is thirsty and has indicated a desire for some of these strange apricots,' said an officer.

Still Tambal did not move, such was his numbed condition after his recent experiences. Now the Prince himself came down from his palanquin and said:

'I am Jadugarzada, son of the magician-king of the East. Here is a bag of gold, oaf. I am having some of your fruit, because I am desirous of it. I am in a hurry, hastening to claim my bride, Princess Precious Pearl, daughter of Kahana, magician-king of the West.'

At these words Tambal's heart turned over. But, realising that this must be his destiny which the sage had told him to follow, he offered the Prince as much of the fruit as he could eat.

When he had eaten, the Prince began to fall asleep. As he did so, horns, fur and huge ears started to grow out of him. The soldiers shook him, and the Prince began to behave in a strange. way. He claimed that *he* was normal, and that *they* were deformed.

The councillors who accompanied the party restrained the prince and held a hurried debate. Tambal claimed that all would have been well if the prince had not fallen asleep. Eventually it was decided to put Tambal in the palanquin to play the part of the prince. The horned Jadugarzada was tied to a horse with a veil thrown over his face, disguised as a serving-woman.

'He may recover his wits eventually,' said the councillors, 'and in any case he is still our Prince. Tambal shall marry the girl. Then, as soon as possible, we shall carry them all back to our own country for our king to unravel the problem.'

Tambal, biding his time and following his destiny, agreed to his own part in the masquerade.

When the party arrived at the capital of the West, the king himself came out to meet them. Tambal was taken to the princess as her bridegroom, and she was so astonished that she nearly fainted. But Tambal managed to whisper to her rapidly what had happened, and they were duly married, amid great jubilations.

In the meantime the horned prince had half recovered his wits, but not his human form, and his escort still kept him under cover. As soon as the feasting was over, the chief of the horned prince's party (who had been keeping Tambal and the princess under a very close watch) presented himself to the court. He said: 'O just and glorious monarch, fountain of wisdom; the time has now come, according to the pronouncements of our astrologers and sooth-sayers, to conduct the bridal pair back to our own land, so that they may be established in their new home under the most felicitous circumstances and influences.'

The princess turned to Tambal in alarm, for she knew that Jadugarzada would claim her as soon as they were on the open road – and make an end of Tambal into the bargain.

Tambal whispered to her, 'Fear nothing. We must act as best

we can, following our destiny. Agree to go, making only the condition that you will not travel without the wooden horse.'

At first the magician-king was annoyed at this foible of his daughter's. He realised that she wanted the horse because it was connected with her first suitor. But the chief minister of the horned prince said: 'Majesty, I cannot see that this is anything worse than a whim for a toy, such as any young girl might have. I hope that you will allow her to have her plaything, so that we may make haste homeward.'

So the magician-king agreed, and soon the cavalcade was resplendently on its way. After the king's escort had withdrawn, and before the time of the first night-halt, the hideous Jadugarzada threw off his veil and cried out to Tambal:

'Miserable author of my misfortunes! I now intend to bind you hand and foot, to take you captive back to my own land. If, when we arrive there, you do not tell me how to remove this enchantment, I will have you flayed alive, inch by inch. Now, give me the Princess Precious Pearl.'

Tambal ran to the princess and, in front of the astonished party, rose into the sky on the wooden horse with Precious Pearl mounted behind him.

Within a matter of minutes the couple alighted at the palace of King Mumkin. They related everything that had happened to them, and the king was almost overcome with delight at their safe return. He at once gave orders for the hapless woodcarver to be released, recompensed and applauded by the entire populace.

When the king was gathered to his fathers, Princess Precious Pearl and Prince Tambal succeeded him. Prince Hoshyar was quite pleased, too, because he was still entranced by the wondrous fish.

'I am glad for your own sakes, if you are happy,' he used to say to them, 'but, for my own part, nothing is more rewarding than concerning myself with the wondrous fish.'

And this history is the origin of a strange saying current among the people of that land, yet whose beginnings have now been forgotten. The saying is: 'Those who want fish can achieve much through fish, and those who do not know their heart's desire may first have to hear the story of the wooden horse.'

The Prince of Darkness

ONCE upon a time, in the city of Damascus, there lived a goldsmith. He made items of jewellery so finely that his fame spread even to the ears of Eblis, the Evil One.

The goldsmith was sitting in his shop one day, finishing the wings of a golden butterfly, when he saw the dark-visaged Evil One looking through the window.

'Allah have mercy upon me!' cried the goldsmith. 'Has my last hour come?'

The door opened as if pushed by invisible hands, and the tall black-robed figure entered.

The Evil One smiled and said:

'Good fellow, have no fear, I have not come for you. I was merely looking at your wonderful handiwork. I have heard, even in the lower regions, of your exquisite craftsmanship. I would like to have some samples, shall we say the few pieces which you have in the window?'

'Why, yes certainly, have all you please,' said the goldsmith willingly. He was so glad that the Evil One was going to spare him that he would have given anything. 'I will wrap them up and you shall take them at once. There is a jewelled bear, a golden fish with ruby eyes, and a necklace fit for a . . .'

'No, no,' said the Evil One impatiently, 'I do not want them now, I will come back for them another time. Keep all that there is in the window for me, even though I may be years in returning. Will you promise?'

'I promise,' said the goldsmith, and the Evil One vanished.

'Who was that talking to you?' asked the goldsmith's wife, bringing her husband a glass of sherbet.

'My dear,' said he, 'it was no other than Eblis the accursed Prince of Darkness himself. He made me promise to keep everything which I have in the window for him, which he will come back to collect when he is ready. Though I grieve for my beautiful pieces of handiwork, I am grateful that (thanks to the Mercy of Allah) he has not carried me off to Jehannum.'

'Everything in the window?'

'That was what the Evil One said.'

At that moment the woman clapped her hands to her head and began to weep.

'Alas, alas, our child was playing in the window, and that means that the Evil One means to take her too when he comes back!' she said.

The goldsmith rushed to have a look, and sure enough, there was his little daughter, innocently playing with the golden toys which her father had put on show.

'Quick, wife,' said he, 'go to the silversmith's, and bring me an ounce of virgin silver.' His wife did as she was bid, and brought back the silver, crying into her kerchief.

The goldsmith went to his workshop, and taking the holy Koran from the shelf, read the Throne-Verse from it. Then he hammered out the silver as thin as paper and engraved a talisman for his daughter to wear around her neck.

For he knew that a charm was most potent if worked in silver, and he told his daughter that she must never take off the talisman or Eblis could carry her away.

Years passed, and still the Evil One did not come back. The goldsmith and his wife had almost forgotten about the matter when suddenly the Evil One appeared again in the goldsmith's shop.

'I have come for my treasures as you promised,' said the Evil One, 'And the girl must now be about seventeen, is she not?'

'Yes,' said the goldsmith, 'But change your mind, O Mighty Eblis, about our daughter, she is the only child of our old age. I beg you, please, please spare her. Take me instead, I am beyond the pleasures of life, but she is young. Take me, great prince of darkness!'

'No, no no, I cannot possibly do that,' said the Evil One, dashing aside the beautiful golden figures which the goldsmith handed him, 'I want her especially . . . '

So the goldsmith sent the servant to ask his daughter to come, as she was required urgently.

Now, the girl, whose name was Zorah, was taking a bath, and

in her haste to do her father's bidding, she forgot to put on her talismanic necklace when she dressed. She ran to the shop, but there was something about the tall dark stranger with her father which made her shrink away from him.

'Zorah, my child,' said the goldsmith, 'this is Eblis, the mighty ruler of the lower regions, who has come to take you away with him.' Thinking that his daughter was protected by the silver talisman, the goldsmith continued: 'But as you have your talisman around your neck you need not go, so have no fear.'

'What!' the Evil One cried. 'How dare you try to trick me? I will not be robbed like this!' and he reached out his hand to grasp the girl's clothing, but she ran away so quickly that her veil was left in his claw-like fingers. Zorah ran as fast as her feet would carry her, and found her talisman beside the bath. She put it on, and was protected from the Evil One immediately. Eblis gave a cry of rage, and said to the goldsmith 'All right, I am going now, but I will be back for your daughter in seven days, mark my words!' And he vanished to make certain arrangements with his fiends.

Now, the goldsmith thought of a plan, and it was this: that he should make a waxen model of his daughter, and conceal a machine inside the body, so that it could walk and talk like a human being.

He worked secretly in the cellar for seven days and seven nights, until he had made a perfect replica of his daughter, so complete that even her mother could hardly tell the difference.

Then, having sent the girl away to her aunt's house in a nearby village, the goldsmith awaited his diabolical visitor.

Sure enough, as he was sitting in his workshop, the Evil One appeared once more, and said 'Bring your daughter hither this instant, old man, without her talisman, or I will set my fiends to burn your house down. I am in no mood to be trifled with at the moment.'

The goldsmith put his head behind the curtains which led to the women's apartments and said 'Zorah my child, come out at once, for the mighty Eblis, Prince of Darkness, has come for you.'

When she heard her husband's words, the goldsmith's wife turned the key in the back of the beautiful life-sized doll, and arranged a rose-pink veil around its head. 'I hear and obey, father,' she said in a gentle voice and parted the curtains, giving the doll a push. Then she hid herself and waited.

The goldsmith held his breath as he saw the lovely creature glide into the room.

When Eblis the Evil One glimpsed the shrouded figure he called:

'Come to me now, beautiful mortal, so that I may take you with me to my wonderful kingdom of darkness. There you shall be my queen of eternal night.' He pulled off the pink veil, and saw a pair of modestly lowered lashes. The voice of the doll murmured softly 'I hear and obey, Prince of Darkness.'

So the Evil One snatched the image up in his arms and bore it away to the lower regions.

Now, that night there was a great feast in the kingdom of ever-lasting fire, for Eblis had previously instructed his minions to prepare everything of the finest for the night's entertainment.

The food was wonderful, the wine was perfect, the music was gay. But, unfortunately, the fire was just a little too hot. While the Evil One was sitting and drinking merrily on his ebony throne, the wax maiden started to melt, and fell into the flames. The model was devoured in an instant. The fiends stood aghast, and leant on their pitchforks, wondering how their devilish master was going to take his loss.

To their great relief he cried out 'Well, these humans are a fragile lot. That wretched girl had only been with us a short while. What chance had she of lasting down here as my bride for eternity? I was mistaken. Build up the fire!'

And the party became merrier, and the wine flowed, while the great fire crackled louder than every before. The feast went on far into the night, and the Evil One never thought of Zorah, the goldsmith's daughter, again.

Encounter at a Hermitage

This story is said to have been told one day by Emir Hamza (died 1710) in answer to the question: 'In what manner could you relate to us an equivalence of your power to live in a world other than ours?'

It is related that he could 'slip into invisibility just by taking a sideways step, when his feet were at right angles to one another.' About this, as about other wonders, he said: 'I forbid you to relate any wonder of mine without adding that the performance of wonders is for a purpose of self-improvement or passing power, not amazement or faith, to others.'

Another remark made by Hamza is: 'We go to another land, in form and fancy, sometimes really remaining here; but sometimes literally.

'From this world we bring back what you need; food that has never been tasted, drink that has never been swallowed.'

Shah Firoz died in 1660, and in popular repute is still alive, in a new form, as one of the Hidden Guides of the Sufis.

I HAD walked to a hermitage in the Hindu Kush to visit its Sheikh, and also to see if I could find some way of stilling my doubts about some way of proving the real existence of the Hidden Path. It was only after many adventures that I at last came across the friendly sight of smoke rising through the chimney-hole of that simple building.

A man, plainly dressed, an honest expression on his face, was sitting quietly at the door of the hermitage.

He said, 'Welcome, brother.' Far from feeling glad, I was disturbed to find so little respect for me in this man, who was surely the watchman.

'Are you the watchman?' I asked.

'I am called that,' he said.

'I am looking for the Ancient, the Guide ' I told him.

'I am called that,' he answered.

And then I was glad that the great teacher had called me brother. As we went into the house a small dog ran to the Sheikh's side, delighted that he had come back.

'Welcome, brother,' said the Sheikh to the animal, and I was again downcast to think that by this greeting I had been put on a level with the dog, that I had not been honoured at all. But out of politeness I said nothing, for I was the guest.

Soon we were seated before a bowl of yoghurt; when the Guide spoke, it was to recite a poem.

'A puff of smoke against a mountain – the heart grows glad.
'A kind word to a little dog – the heart grows sad.'

I was amazed that he could understand my secret thoughts in this way, and uneasy, and rather ashamed.

'Teach me,' I said.

He answered, 'What do I sing, and what does my lute sing? You and I are not in harmony, although I understand your thoughts. What have you already taught yourself? What have others taught you? You are uneasy because you have come so far and at the end of your journey have found someone who can read your thoughts. And you feel that perhaps you could learn this power, and then use it to your heart's content. I seem acceptable to you, as people sometimes think of doctrines as being acceptable to them. But are you acceptable to me? People never bother to think that the doctrine may not accept them.'

For the first time I was overcome by real fear; alone with this man of power in such a lonely place, I began to tremble.

And the Guide continued, 'You must go away. You are still too raw for a teacher to develop; a fruit must be touched by the right things, by those elements which ripen it. Go away, strive, work in every possible way. When you are nearer maturity you will be able properly to understand the experience of our master, Ben-Adhem, who gave away the throne of Balkh to be with us.

'For he was walking along the road one day when he saw a stone on the ground. It had written on it, "TURN ME OVER AND READ." So he picked it up and looked at the other side. And there was written, "WHY DO YOU SEEK MORE KNOWLEDGE

ENCOUNTER AT A HERMITAGE

WHEN YOU PAY NO HEED TO WHAT YOU KNOW ALREADY?".'

Turning from the Sage I thought to myself, 'I wish that everyone could have an encounter like this, so that at least it would be common knowledge that teaching of this kind exists in the world.'

He went on, 'Often the penalty of knowledge is to be laughed at. Tell people of our discussion here and they will think you mad. In this way, real knowledge protects itself.'

I made no attempt to shape words, but in my heart, as earnestly as I could, I framed the thought, 'How can I serve?'

And, also without words, Shah Firoz spoke directly to my heart, 'Increase the desire to serve and a chance of service may be given you.'

Only when through frequent effort I had reached this stage did I realise the true value of my encounter with him who is called 'Shah Firoz'.

(Firman-Bardar of Badakhshan).

*   *   *

He who has made a door and a lock, has also made a key.

Saying.

Learn to behave from those who cannot.

Saying.

The Shrine

Described by one commentator as 'A profound allegory of man's capacity for self-deception, rationalising power, and tendency to base one creed on another,' this story is traditionally said to originate with Haji Bektash (died 1337) – founder of the Bektashi Order of Dervishes.

Another opinion of the story is that 'it is intended to show the parallel between real religion and what man understands by it.

Real religion is likened to the tomb of a true saint: what man understands by it is equal to the burying of a donkey instead of a saint.'

Dervishes have been known to press the tale into service in order to ridicule themselves, saying: 'All shrines are a hoax.' They do this for the purpose of discouraging unsuitable candidates for discipleship.

MULLA Nasrudin's father was the highly-respected keeper of a shrine, the burial-place of a great teacher which was a place of pilgrimage attracting the credulous and the Seekers After Truth alike.

In the usual course of events, Nasrudin could be expected to inherit this position. But soon after his fifteenth year, when he was considered to be a man, he decided to follow the ancient maxim: 'Seek knowledge, even if it be in China.'

'I will not try to prevent you, my son,' said his father. So Nasrudin saddled a donkey and set off on his travels.

He visited the lands of Egypt and Babylon, roamed in the Arabian Desert, struck northward to Iconium, to Bokhara, Samarkand and the Hindu-Kush mountains, consorting with dervishes and always heading towards the farthest East.

Nasrudin was struggling across the mountain ranges in Kashmir after a detour through Little Tibet when, overcome by the rarefied atmosphere and privations, his donkey lay down and died.

THE SHRINE

Nasrudin was overcome with grief; for this was the only constant companion of his journeyings, which had covered a period of a dozen years or more. Heartbroken, he buried his friend and raised a simple mound over the grave. There he remained in silent meditation; the towering mountains above him, and the rushing torrents below.

Before very long people who were taking the mountain road between India and Central Asia, China and the shrines of Turkestan, observed this lonely figure: alternately weeping at his loss and gazing across the valleys of Kashmir.

'This must indeed be the grave of a holy man,' they said to one another; 'and a man of no mean accomplishments, if his disciple mourns him thus. Why, he has been here for many months, and his grief shows no sign of abating.'

Presently a rich man passed, and gave orders for a dome and shrine to be erected on the spot, as a pious act. Other pilgrims terraced the mountainside and planted crops whose produce went to the upkeep of the shrine. The fame of the Silent Mourning Dervish spread until Nasrudin's father came to hear of it. He at once set off on a pilgrimage to the sanctified spot. When he saw Nasrudin he asked him what had happened. Nasrudin told him. The old dervish raised his hands in amazement:

'Know, O my son,' he exclaimed, 'that the shrine where you were brought up and which you abandoned was raised in exactly the same manner, by a similar chain of events, when my own donkey died, over thirty years ago.'

* * *

Salt is not attacked by ants.

Proverb.

Mushkil Gusha

When a number of people come together, and if these people are harmonised in a certain way, excluding some who make for disharmony – we have what we call an event. *This is by no means what is generally understood in contemporary cultures as an event. For them, something which takes place and which impresses people by means of subjective impacts – is called an event. This is what some term a 'lesser event', because it takes place in the lesser world, that of human relationships easily produced, synthesised, commemorated.*

The real event, of which the lesser event is a useful similitude (not more and no less) is that which belongs to the higher realm.

We cannot accurately render a higher event in stilted terrestrial representations and retain accuracy. Something of surpassing importance in a higher realm could not entirely be put in terms of literature, science, or drama, without loss of essential value. But certain tales, providing that they contain elements from the high-event area which may seem absurd, unlikely, improbable or even defective, can (together with the presence of certain people) communicate to the necessary area of the mind the higher event.

Why should it be valuable to do so? Because familiarity with the 'high event', however produced, enables the individual's mind to operate in the high realm.

The tale of Mushkil Gusha is an example. The very 'lack of completeness' in the events, the 'untidiness' of the theme, the absence of certain factors which we have come to expect in a story: these in this case are indications of the greater parallel.

The Story of Mushkil Gusha

ONCE upon a time, not a thousand miles from here, there lived a poor old wood-cutter, who was a widower, and his little daughter. He used to go every day into the mountains to cut firewood which he brought home and tied into bundles. Then he used to have breakfast and walk into the nearest town, where he would sell his wood and rest for a time before returning home.

One day, when he got home very late, the girl said to him, 'Father, I sometimes wish that we could have some nicer food, and more and different kinds of things to eat.'

'Very well, my child,' said the old man; 'tomorrow I shall get up much earlier than I usually do. I shall go further into the mountains where there is more wood, and I shall bring back a much larger quantity than usual. I will get home earlier and I will be able to bundle the wood sooner, and I will go into town and sell it so that we can have more money and I shall bring you back all kinds of nice things to eat.'

The next morning the wood-cutter rose before dawn and went into the mountains. He worked very hard cutting wood and trimming it and made it into a huge bundle which he carried on his back to his little house.

When he got home, it was still very early. He put his load of wood down, and knocked on the door, saying, 'Daughter, Daughter, open the door, for I am hungry and thirsty and I need a meal before I go to market.'

But the door was locked. The wood-cutter was so tired that he lay down and was soon fast asleep beside his bundle. The little girl, having forgotten all about their conversation the night before, was fast asleep in bed. When he woke up a few hours later, the sun was high. The wood-cutter knocked on the door again and said, 'Daughter, Daughter, come quickly; I must have a little food and go to market to sell the wood; for it is already much later than my usual time of starting.'

But, having forgotten all about the conversation the night

before, the little girl had meanwhile got up, tidied the house, and gone out for a walk. She had locked the door assuming in her forgetfulness that her father was still in the town.

So the wood-cutter thought to himself, 'It is now rather late to go into the town. I will therefore return to the mountains and cut another bundle of wood, which I will bring home, and tomorrow I will take a double load to market.'

All that day the old man toiled in the mountains cutting wood and shaping the branches. When he got home with the wood on his shoulders, it was evening.

He put down his burden behind the house, knocked on the door and said, 'Daughter, Daughter, open the door for I am tired and I have eaten nothing all day. I have a double bundle of wood which I hope to take to market tomorrow. Tonight I must sleep well so that I will be strong.'

But there was no answer, for the little girl when she came home had felt very sleepy, and had made a meal for herself, and gone to bed. She had been rather worried at first that her father was not at home, but she decided that he must have arranged to stay in the town overnight.

Once again the wood-cutter, finding that he could not get into the house, tired, hungry and thirsty, lay down by his bundles of wood and fell fast asleep. He could not keep awake, although he was fearful for what might have happened to the little girl.

Now the wood-cutter, because he was so cold and hungry and tired, woke very, very early the next morning: before it was even light.

He sat up, and looked around, but he could not see anything. And then a strange thing happened. The wood-cutter thought he heard a voice saying: 'Hurry, hurry! Leave your wood and come this way. If you need enough, and you *want* little enough, you shall have delicious food.'

The wood-cutter stood up and walked in the direction of the voice. And he walked and he walked; but he found nothing.

By now he was colder and hungrier and more tired than ever, and he was lost. He had been full of hope, but that did not seem to have helped him. Now he felt sad, and he wanted to cry. But he realised that crying would not help him either, so he lay down and fell asleep.

Quite soon he woke up again. It was too cold, and he was too hungry, to sleep. So he decided to tell himself, as if in a story, everything that had happened to him since his little daughter had first said that she wanted a different kind of food.

As soon as he had finished his story, he thought he heard another voice, saying, somewhere above him, out of the dawn, 'Old man, what are you doing sitting there?'

'I am telling myself my own story,' said the wood-cutter.

'And what is that?' said the voice.

The old man repeated his tale. 'Very well,' said the voice. And then the voice told the old wood-cutter to close his eyes and to mount as it were, a step. 'But I do not see any step,' said the old man. 'Never mind, but do as I say,' said the voice.

The old man did as he was told. As soon as he had closed his eyes he found that he was standing up and as he raised his right foot he felt that there was something like a step under it. He started to ascend what seemed to be a staircase. Suddenly the whole flight of steps started to move, very fast, and the voice said, 'Do not open your eyes until I tell you to do so.'

In a very short time, the voice told the old man to open his eyes. When he did he found that he was in a place which looked rather like a desert, with the sun beating down on him. He was surrounded by masses and masses of pebbles; pebbles of all colours: red, green, blue and white. But he seemed to be alone. He looked all around him, and could not see anyone, but the voice started to speak again.

'Take up as many of these stones as you can,' said the voice, 'Then close your eyes, and walk down the steps once more.'

The wood-cutter did as he was told, and he found himself, when he opened his eyes again at the voice's bidding, standing before the door of his own house.

He knocked at the door and his little daughter answered it. She asked him where he had been, and he told her, although she could hardly understand what he was saying, it all sounded so confusing.

They went into the house, and the little girl and her father shared the last food which they had, which was a handful of dried dates.

When they had finished, the old man thought that he heard a voice speaking to him again, a voice just like the other one which had told him to climb the stairs.

The voice said, 'Although you may not know it yet, you have been saved by Mushkil Gusha. Remember that Mushkil Gusha is always here. Make sure that every Thursday night you eat some dates and give some to any needy person, and tell the story of Mushkil Gusha. Or give a gift in the name of Mushkil Gusha to someone who will help the needy. Make sure that the story of Mushkil Gusha is never, never forgotten. If you do this, and if this is done by those to whom you tell the story, the people who are in real need will always find their way.'

The wood-cutter put all the stones which he had brought back from the desert in a corner of his little house. They looked very much like ordinary stones, and he did not know what to do with them.

The next day he took his two enormous bundles of wood to the market, and sold them easily for a high price. When he got home he took his daughter all sorts of delicious kinds of food, which she had never tasted before. And when they had eaten it, the old wood-cutter said, 'Now I am going to tell you the whole story of Mushkil Gusha. Mushkil Gusha is "the remover of all difficulties". Our difficulties have been removed through Mushkil Gusha and we must always remember it.'

For nearly a week after that the old man carried on as usual. He went into the mountains, brought back wood, had a meal, took the wood to market and sold it. He always found a buyer without difficulty.

Now the next Thursday came, and, as is the way of men, the wood-cutter forgot to repeat the tale of Mushkil Gusha.

Late that evening, in the house of the wood-cutter's neighbours, the fire had gone out. The neighbours had nothing with which to re-light the fire, and they went to the house of the wood-cutter. They said, 'Neighbour, neighbour, please give us a light from those wonderful lamps of yours which we see shining through the window.'

'What lamps?' said the wood-cutter.

'Come outside,' said the neighbours, 'and see what we mean.'

So the wood-cutter went outside and then he saw, sure enough, all kinds of brilliant lights shining through the window from the inside.

He went back to the house, and saw that the light was streaming from the pile of pebbles which he had put in the corner. But the rays of light were cold, and it was not possible to use them to light a fire. So he went out to the neighbours and said, 'Neighbours, I am sorry, I have no fire.' And he banged the door in their faces. They were annoyed and confused, and went back to their house, muttering. They leave our story here.

The wood-cutter and his daughter quickly covered up the brilliant lights with every piece of cloth they could find, for fear that anyone would see what a treasure they had. The next morning, when they uncovered the stones, they discovered that they were precious, luminous gems.

They took the jewels, one by one, to neighbouring towns, where they sold them for a huge price. Now the wood-cutter decided to build for himself and for his daughter a wonderful palace. They chose a site just opposite the castle of the king of their country. In a very short time a marvellous building had come into being.

Now that particular king had a beautiful daughter, and one day when she got up in the morning, she saw a sort of fairy-tale castle just opposite her father's and she was amazed. She asked her servants, 'Who has built this castle? What right have these people to do such a thing so near to our home?'

The servants went away and made enquiries and they came back and told the story, as far as they could collect it, to the princess.

The princess called for the little daughter of the wood-cutter, for she was very angry with her, but when the two girls met and talked they soon became fast friends. They started to meet every day and went to swim and play in the stream which had been made for the princess by her father. A few days after they first met, the princess took off a beautiful and valuable necklace and hung it up on a tree just beside the stream. She forgot to take it down when they came out of the water, and when she got home she thought it must have been lost.

The princess thought a little and then decided that the daughter of the wood-cutter had stolen her necklace. So she told her father, and he had the wood-cutter arrested; he confiscated the castle and declared forfeit everything that the wood-cutter had. The old man was thrown into prison, and the daughter was put into an orphanage.

As was the custom in that country, after a period of time the wood-cutter was taken from the dungeon and put in the public square, chained to a post, with a sign around his neck. On the sign was written 'This is what happens to those who steal from Kings'.

At first people gathered around him, and jeered and threw things at him. He was most unhappy.

But quite soon, as is the way of men, everyone became used to the sight of the old man sitting there by his post, and took very little notice of him. Sometimes people threw him scraps of food, sometimes they did not.

One day he overheard somebody saying that it was Thursday afternoon. Suddenly, the thought came into his mind that it would soon be the evening of Mushkil Gusha, the remover of all difficulties, and that he had forgotten to commemorate him for so many days. No sooner had this thought come into his head, than a charitable man, passing by, threw him a tiny coin. The wood-cutter called out: 'Generous friend, you have given me money, which is of no use to me. If, however, your kindness could extend to buying one or two dates and coming and sitting and eating them with me, I would be eternally grateful to you.'

The other man went and bought a few dates. And they sat and ate them together. When they had finished, the wood-cutter told the other man the story of Mushkil Gusha. 'I think you must be mad,' said the generous man. But he was a kindly person who himself had many difficulties. When he arrived home after this incident, he found that all his problems had disappeared. And that made him start to think a great deal about Mushkil Gusha. But he leaves our story here.

The very next morning the princess went back to her bathing-place. As she was about to go into the water, she saw what looked like her necklace down at the bottom of the stream. As she was going to dive in to try to get it back, she happened to sneeze. Her head went up, and she saw that what she had thought was the necklace was only its reflection in the water. It was hanging on the bough of the tree where she had left it such a long time before. Taking the necklace down, the princess ran excitedly to her father and told him what had happened. The King gave orders for the wood-cutter to be released and given a public apology. The little girl was brought back from the orphanage, and everyone lived happily ever after.

These are some of the incidents in the story of Mushkil Gusha. It is a very long tale and it is never ended. It has many forms. Some of them are even not called the story of Mushkil Gusha at all, so people do not recognise it. But it is because of Mushkil Gusha that his story, in whatever form, is remembered by somebody, somewhere in the world, day and night, wherever there are people. As his story had always been recited, so it will always continue to be told.

Will *you* repeat the story of Mushkil Gusha on Thursday nights, and help the work of Mushkil Gusha?

* * *

A hand and a foot do not clap together.

Proverb.

Cheating Death

ONCE there was a man called Omar, who was a most wealthy merchant. He had a fleet of fine ships, bringing merchandise from far lands. His line was noble, his honour unsullied.

One day, his good fortune deserted him. News came that in a fierce storm all his ships had been wrecked, his sailors drowned to a man.

'Allah have mercy upon me!' cried Omar, 'Surely this is the worst day of my life.' But more was to come. Upon returning to his house, he found that it had been burned to the ground, his stocks of silks and jewels gone, his gold taken by thieves. The servants, unable to face him, had run away. He was alone, no money, no home, no personal possessions.

'Without my treasures I am finished,' he thought, 'I cannot bear to hold up my head among those who respected me for my wealth and position. How in my agony can I start again? It is impossible.' And so he decided to take his courage in his hands, and cast himself from a high rock into the sea. The angry waters closed over his head, and he fell as if into a bottomless pit.

But the sea, after half-drowning him, cast him up on to the sands. There he lay, blinking up at the sun, in torn and filthy clothes, unable to believe that he was still alive.

'I only want to die,' he cried to the unheeding sky, 'I can no longer live.'

He picked himself up, and staggered through the rocks upon the beach, thinking of many ways to take his life.

In the streets of the town where he wandered, half-crazed with despair, no one knew him for the once-great merchant that he used to be. He was jostled, pushed out of the way, shouted at by little boys.

Suddenly, there was an outcry. 'Death to all kings and rulers!' Omar heard the voice of a mad, ragged beggar who was brandishing a knife. He stopped to see what was happening. It was at the gate of the royal palace, where the captain of the guard lay dead, slain by the madman.

CHEATING DEATH

The soldiers seemed powerless to stop the huge beggar, and Omar ran swiftly to help the king, as the shining blade rose again in the insane beggar's hand. Without fear, Omar grappled with the man, and they rolled over and over on the marble floor. The guards rushed into the throne-room, and severed the madman's head from his shoulders.

'Stop,' said the king, as Omar tried to run away, bent on finding some other way to bring about his own destruction. 'Come here, my good fellow, for I must reward you for saving my life.'

'Your Majesty,' said Omar, 'I wish for no reward, I only wish to die.'

'Die?' said the king, 'Why should you die? Tell me all, omitting no detail.'

'My ships have all been wrecked, my house burned, my gold stolen by thieves. I can no longer hold up my head among my associates, therefore I must find the quickest way to leave this unhappy world. Even the sea refused to drown me.'

'Foolish man,' said the king, 'for saving my life you shall benefit. Is it not forbidden to commit the great sin of taking one's own life? Come, you shall regain all you have lost, and become once more high in the land.'

The king gave instructions to his Grand Vizier then that Omar was to receive a robe of honour, new ships were to be fitted out for him, regardless of cost, and all his gold restored from the royal treasury.

From that hour Omar became once more respected and honoured and lost the desire to die.

In time he became so wealthy that he was able to ask for the king's daughter in marriage, and amassed a vast fortune in fabulous merchandise.

One day, he was walking in his rose garden, smelling one particularly beautiful bloom, when he heard a voice calling his name. He turned, and saw a tall figure, with covered face and folded hands, standing under a tree.

'Peace be upon you!' said Omar. 'Whom have I the pleasure of greeting?'

'I am the Angel of Death,' said the shrouded figure, 'And I have come to take you to Paradise. You must come with me now.'

'Oh, no, no, I cannot come with you,' said Omar, 'I am not ready to go now. I have a fine rich life, everything I need, the king's daughter for my wife. Please spare me, let me enjoy the good things of this wonderful world a little longer.'

'You must come with me,' said the Angel of Death. 'I have my duty, just like anyone else. Come, for I must be off to take the call to other men as well.'

Then Omar thought of a crafty plan.

'I am not prepared,' he said. 'Let me go to the mosque, and say my prayers, then I will come with you willingly.'

'After you have said your prayers you will come with me? You promise?' asked the Angel.

'Yes, I promise,' said Omar, and bent his head to hide a smile.

The Angel vanished, and Omar laughed aloud.

And from that day Omar never went near a mosque.

Years passed, and Omar became more and more important. When his first grey hairs had come he peered at himself in a looking glass and thought 'How distinguished I have become, surely I am the most important person in the land after my respected father-in-law, the king.'

A servant entered at that moment to say that the king requested Omar's presence at court before the hour was gone.

Omar hastened to listen to what the king had to say. 'My dear Omar,' said the monarch, 'the religious teacher of the Turquoise Mosque has died, and I can think of no one more suitable than yourself to take his place. Come, let us go together, this being Friday, and you shall lead the prayer at midday.'

'No, no, Your Majesty!' said Omar in anguish, 'I—I am not worthy, please choose someone else, anyone but me.'

'Your modesty does you credit,' said the king, 'but I am now even more decided that it shall be you. Let us hurry, for it is nearly twelve.' Attended by the courtiers, the king and Omar walked towards the Turquoise Mosque.

Although the sun overhead was hot, Omar felt as if an icy hand clutched at his heart. His pride left him, and he knew that the Angel of Death was not far away. They reached the mosque, and Omar led the congregation in prayer. As the Faithful bent their knees, and rose, and knelt again, Omar prayed more fervently to

Allah than he had ever done before. He beseeched the Almighty to forgive his great sins in life, and have compassion.

After a few moments, the Angel of Death, with covered head and folded hands, appeared to Omar, unseen by the rest.

'Come with me now,' said the Angel, 'I have waited a long time for you, and this is your day of reckoning.'

All at once Omar felt a great peace within his heart. He inclined his head. 'Very well,' he said, 'it is a great relief after all, to see you at last. I will go with you. Paradise after all is the just reward for all True Believers after this life on Earth.'

'No, not so,' said the Angel. 'I am not here to take you to Paradise. I came before to do so, but you tricked me, remember, and now you are to be punished. You are to be sent to the lower regions, for you have had your paradise on Earth.'

Before Omar could utter a cry the Angel of Death embraced him in his chilly arms and bore him away, leaving upon the marble floor a lifeless figure, clad in a priceless robe, kneeling as if in prayer.

* * *

A nut has a sweet kernel: a date has a useless stone.

Proverb.

No answer is in itself an answer.

Proverb.

The Three Perceptives

THERE were once three Sufis, so observant and experienced in life that they were known as The Three Perceptives.

One day during their travels they encountered a camelman, who said: 'Have you seen my camel? I have lost it.'

'Was it blind in one eye?' asked the first Perceptive.

'Yes,' said the cameldriver.

'Has it one tooth missing in front?' asked the second Perceptive.

'Yes, yes,' said the cameldriver.

'Is it lame in one foot?' asked the third Perceptive.

'Yes, yes, yes,' said the cameldriver.

The three Perceptives then told the man to go back along the way they had come, and that he might hope to find it. Thinking that they had seen it, the man hurried on his way.

But the man did not find his camel, and he hastened to catch up with the Perceptives, hoping that they would tell him what to do.

He found them that evening, at a resting-place.

'Has your camel honey on one side and a load of corn on the other?' asked the first Perceptive.

'Yes,' said the man.

'Is there a pregnant woman mounted upon it?' asked the second Perceptive.

'Yes, yes,' said the man.

'We do not know where it is,' said the third Perceptive.

The cameldriver was now convinced that the Perceptives had stolen his camel, passenger and all, and he took them to the judge, accusing them of the theft.

The Judge thought that he had made out a case, and detained the three men in custody on suspicion of theft.

A little later, the man found his camel wandering in some fields, and returning to the court, arranged for the Perceptives to be released.

The judge, who had not given them a chance to explain themselves before, asked how it was that they knew so much about the camel, since they had apparently not even seen it.

'We saw the footprints of a camel on the road,' said the first Perceptive.

'One of the tracks was faint: it must have been lame,' said the second Perceptive.

'It had stripped the bushes at only one side of the road, so it must have been blind in one eye,' said the third Perceptive.

'The leaves were shredded, which indicated the loss of a tooth,' continued the first Perceptive.

'Bees and ants, on different sides of the road, were swarming over something deposited; we saw that this was honey and corn,' said the second Perceptive.

'We found long human hair where someone had stopped and dismounted, it was a woman's,' said the third Perceptive.

'Where the person had sat down there were palm-prints, we thought from the use of the hands that the woman was probably very pregnant and had to stand up in that way,' said the first Perceptive.

'Why did you not apply for your side of the case to be heard so that you could explain yourselves?' asked the judge.

'Because we reckoned that the cameldriver would continue looking for his camel and might find it soon,' said the first Perceptive.

'He would feel generous in releasing us through his discovery,' said the second Perceptive.

'The curiosity of the Judge would prompt an enquiry,' said the third Perceptive.

'Discovering the truth by his own enquiries would be better for all than for us to claim that we had been impatiently handled,' said the first Perceptive.

'It is our experience that it is generally better for people to arrive at truth through what they take to be their own volition,' said the second Perceptive.

'It is time for us to move on, for there is work to be done,' said the third Perceptive.

And the Sufi thinkers went on their way. They are still to be found at work on the highways of the earth.

Extracts

Definitions from Mulla Do-Piaza

Reporter · A cat waiting at a mousehole.

Sickness · The messenger of death.

Debtor · A donkey in a quagmire.

Community · Irrationals unified by hope of the impossible.

Patience · A support for the disappointed.

Sword of God · The empty stomachs of the poor.

Worry · Something to make you unnecessarily ill.

Mirror · A means of laughing in your own face.

Drugs · Source of the mystical experience of the ignorant.

A test · A hardship you do not expect

Poverty · The result of marriage.

Intellectual · One who knows no craft.

Penitent · Someone who has been made incapable of enjoying himself.

Wisdom · Something you can learn without knowing it.

A fool · A man trying to be honest with the dishonest.

Brave man · Someone looking for a test.

Friends · Material substances.

Emotionalist · A man or woman who thinks he has experienced the the divine.

Poet · A beggar with pride.

Supporter · Someone who will say anything.

Bribe · Substitute for law, which is a substitute for justice.

Truthful man · He who is, secretly, regarded by everyone as an enemy.

Flattery · One of the most promising of businesses: always brisk.

Adherent   Someone who will believe anything except what he
            should.

            The Mulla's definitions form contemplation materials
            rather than aphorisms. The reader is supposed to be
            able to interpret each saying in several different
            ways. As an example, the message about the Fool
            may mean: 'Don't be honest with the dishonest' – or
            it may mean 'Don't try to be honest: *be* honest.'
            Most people tend to interpret the sayings defensively.
            This, says Do-Piaza, 'is the first step towards not
            being defensive.'

                        *   *   *

            He discards a quilt for fear of bugs.
                                                Proverb.

            If you have no troubles – buy a goat.   •
                                                Proverb.

The Two Brothers

THERE were once two brothers who jointly farmed a field, and always shared its yield.

One day one of them woke up in the night and thought:

'My brother is married and has children. Because of this he has anxieties and expenses which are not mine. So I will go and move some sacks from my share into his storeroom, which is only fair. I shall do this under cover of night, so that he may not, from his generosity, dispute with me about it.'

He moved the sacks, and went back to bed.

Soon afterwards the other brother woke up and thought to himself:

'It is not fair that I should have half of all the corn in our field. My brother, who is unmarried, lacks my pleasures in having a family, and I shall therefore try to compensate a little by moving some of my corn into his storeroom.'

So saying, he did so.

The next morning, each was amazed that he still had the same number of sacks in his storeroom, and afterwards neither could understand why, year after year, the number of sacks remained the same even when each of them shifted some by stealth.

* * *

Be a dog, but don't be a younger brother.

Proverb.

The Angel and the Charitable Man

ONE day a venerable hermit who had spent many years in contemplation and isolation received a visit from a celestial creature.

Now, he felt, here was a result of his austerities, a confirmation that he was progressing on the road to sanctity.

'Hermit,' said the angel, 'you are to go and tell a certain charitable man that it has been decreed by the Most High that because of his good works he is to die in exactly six months from now and to be taken straight to paradise.'

Delighted, the hermit hurried to the house of the charitable man.

When he heard the message the charitable man immediately increased the amount of his benefactions, hoping that he could help more people, even though he had already been promised paradise.

But three whole years passed, and the charitable man did not die. He continued his work unconcerned.

But the hermit, feeling frustrated that his prediction had not turned out to be true, annoyed because it seemed after all that he had had a mere hallucination, stung because people pointed him out in the street as a false prophet and pretended recipient of visitants, was becoming more and more sour, until nobody could stand his company, least of all himself.

Then the angel appeared again.

'You see,' it said, 'how frail a thing you are. True enough, the charitable man has gone to paradise, and has in fact 'died' in a certain manner known only to the elect, while he yet enjoys this life. But you, you are still almost worthless. Now that you have felt the stings which vanity brings on, perhaps you will be able to make a start on the road to spirituality.'

Hospitality

THE people of Turkestan are renowned for their generosity, their self-respect and their love of horses.

A certain Turkestani, called Anwar Beg, once owned a beautiful, fast-pacing and highly pedigreed horse. Everyone coveted it, but he refused to sell, no matter the price offered.

Time and again a friend of his, a horse-dealer named Yakub, visited Anwar, in the hope that he might buy the horse. Anwar always declined to sell.

One day, hearing that Anwar had fallen upon hard times, Yakub said to himself: 'I will go to Anwar now. Surely he will part with the horse, for such is its value that the sale will restore his fortunes.'

He lost no time in making his way to his friend's house.

As is the custom in that country, Anwar welcomed Yakub, and before any business was discussed there was the matter of the traditional hospitality. A meal was set before them, and they ate it with relish.

When, at length, Yakub was able to broach the subject of his visit, the penniless Anwar said:

'It is not now possible for us to have a discussion on the affair of the horse. Hospitality comes first; and, since you visited me in my poverty and I had to entertain you – know that we had to kill the horse to provide a meal, discharging in the best possible manner the obligations of host.'

The Mongols

WHEN Samarkand was destroyed by the Mongol hordes, those who were not killed in the fighting fled to the East and West. Many reached only death in the desert. Famine, pestilence, the cruel horsemen of Mongolia destroyed many more: men, women and even children.

It is estimated that, apart from those who fell in battle, thirty million people were killed by the Khans who swore that they would wipe from the earth all who did not belong to their race.

Khwaja Anis, the dervish teacher at whose settlement in Afghanistan many refugees sought shelter, spoke to them thus:

'You blame the Mongols. But your own habits and disunity have at least in part been responsible. This scourge has been, at least in part, called forth by the operation of your own folly, accumulating over the centuries.

'You have lost a battle, and you think that you have lost a war. The Mongols are exhilarated and triumphant, crow with derision at your very name, make the people of all the surrounding lands, and even countries far away, cry out in delight at your discomfiture or blind to your misery.

'The Mongols have displaced you from your own houses, have taken your flocks and your land, seem to stand everywhere full of valour and success. Men call you women and cowards.

'In spite of your shortcomings and the belief of your detractors in your feebleness, you will prevail. I announce to you a law of peoples, which has never been negated.

'You and your children will be witnesses to the humbling of these alien oppressors. Their humbling will be such that they will completely disappear. The world of Islam will rise again, and the Mongols in Turkestan, in Khorasan, in Iran and in all the other countries which they have taken will remain only a memory.

'Even among those who delight at their victories today, none will weep at their dissolving. That which seems most impossible at the moment is precisely what will come to pass.'

(*Recitals of Khwaja Anis*).

Letter from a Queen

Mahmud of Ghazna was a great Afghan conqueror of the tenth century whose very name struck terror into the hearts of the Persians and the Indians.

When the ruler of Persian Iraq died, his wife Seada took over the province as regent. Mahmud wrote to her demanding tribute, under the threat of invasion.

This is the letter which the Queen-Mother sent back to Ghazni:

'While my husband was alive I was in fear of the great king Mahmud, who has overrun Persia and India. Now I have no fear. I know that such a monarch would never send an army to combat a woman.

If he were to fight me, I would resist to the end. If I were to win, I would be renowned for evermore. But if the Sultan Mahmud were to prevail – men would merely say that he had defeated an old woman.

Because I realise that the Sultan is too wise a man to lay himself open to either of these alternatives, I am not afraid of what may happen.'

Sultan Mahmud the Idol-Breaker, when he read this message, was so impressed that he swore never to invade Iraq while the Queen lived.

* * *

You will never reach Mecca, I fear: for you are on the road to Turkestan.

Proverb.

The Artillery

MY great-great grandfather, Sayed Jan-Fishan Khan, was invited to India and a great military display was put on for him.

It was intended to illustrate to this independent Afghan chief that the warlike capacities of the British Empire were such that it would be to his advantage to respect it.

An artillery officer was attached to the Khan at one point, and he shouted enthusiastically, drawing the chief's attention every time the shells hit their targets.

This man and several others were subsequently invited back to Paghman, to be the guests of Jan-Fisham Khan.

As they were sitting at the banquet a man came up to Jan-Fishan Khan and said something. As soon as he had answered him, Jan-Fishan turned to the British officers and said, apparently in excitement: 'Did you hear that?'

'What did he say?' they asked.

'It is not "what did he say",' said the Khan, 'but the fact that I understood him and he understood me!'

The officers were nonplussed.

The following day, Jan-Fishan took his guests on a tour of his stables. He pointed out some horses.

One of the horses was being fed. 'Look, how he eats!' roared the Khan.

Another was being exercised. 'He can actually walk, and run!' the Khan exulted, clapping his hands.

The visitors thought that their host must be mad.

They were unable to fathom his extraordinary behaviour until he had to say, as they were leaving: 'You have seen, gentlemen, if you have guns which do exactly what they were designed to do – hitting the target – I, too, am surrounded by things which also appear to be fulfilling their function quite adequately. What I have learned from you is to get excited about it.'

Jan-Fishan Khan's Favour

A MAN came to Jan-Fishan Khan, the mystic and warlord of the Hindu-Kush, known for his ability to suit his behaviour to any situation.

'I have a small favour to ask,' he said.

'Throw him out!' shouted the Khan, 'until he learns that you insult Jan-Fishan by asking him for anything small!'

* * *

What goes into a salt-mine becomes salt.

Proverb.

Man has less than he suspects of: Time, Friends, Hopes, Qualities.

Proverb.

Omar and the Wine-drinker

THE Caliph Omar used to slip out of his house and walk through the streets in disguise, to make sure that justice was being done: a practise followed later by Haroun el-Raschid of Baghdad.

One night he heard some singing, and climbed the wall of a house to see what was going on. He saw a man drinking wine.

Stepping through the window he cried out to the man:

'Are you not ashamed to indulge in what is forbidden in the Koran? Do you think that God cannot see you as you sin?'

The man immediately said:

'Caliph of Islam! I have committed one sin and I admit it. You have, however, in accusing me, sinned thrice. What about your own repentance?'

Omar was taken aback, and asked: 'What sins?'

The man replied:

'The Prophet has forbidden eavesdropping, and you have done that. The Koran says: "Enter a house only after calling a salutation upon the occupants" and you have not done that. It has been laid down that all believers must enter a house through its door, and you have failed to do that.'

Omar accepted the rebuke.

*   *   *

The ways of Allah are wonderful: He had Hell, yet he created India.

Proverb.

The Proper Channels

THE Caliph Marwan was approached by a beggar, who asked him for charity.

'Address your application to Allah,' said Marwan.

'The application has been sent. It came back marked: "Refer to Marwan",' said the beggar.

'Here at last,' said the Caliph, 'is a man who realises that everything must have a channel. It would be well if all you people here present were to realise it.'

The beggar was rewarded.

*   *   *

No colour comes after black.
Proverb.

To send a kiss by messenger.
Saying.

In Spain

In the West, the Omeyya of Spain supported with equal pomp (to those of Baghdad) the title of Commander of the Faithful.

Three miles from Cordova, in honour of his favourite Sultana, the third and greatest of the Abdel-Rahmans (who died in 961) constructed the city palace and gardens of Medina al-Zahara.

Twenty-five years and above three millions sterling were employed by the founder. His liberal taste invited the artists of Constantinople, the most skilful sculptors and architects of the age, and the buildings were sustained or adorned by 1,200 columns of Spanish and African, of Greek and Italian marble.

The Hall of Audience was encrusted with gold and pearls, and a great basin in the centre was surrounded by the curious and costly figures of birds and quadrupeds.

In a lofty pavilion of the gardens one of those basins and fountains, so delightful in a sultry climate, was replenished not with water but with the purest quicksilver.

The seraglio of Abdel-Rahman, his wives, concubines and black eunuchs, amounted to 6,300 persons; and he was attended to the field by a guard of 12,000 horse whose belts and scimitars were studded with gold.

* * *

You make *me* a sinner if you stop me giving you hospitality.

Saying.

Baghdad

MECCA was the patrimony of the line (A.D. 750–960) of Hashim, yet the Abbassids were never tempted to reside either in the birthplace (Mecca) nor the city (Medina) of the Prophet. Damascus was disgraced by the choice, and polluted by the blood, of the Omeyya. After some hesitation Al-Mansur, the brother and successor of Saffah, laid the foundations of Baghdad, the imperial seat of his posterity during a reign of 500 years.

The chosen spot is on the eastern bank of the Tigris about fifteen miles above the ruins of Modain. The double wall was of a circular form; and such was the rapid increase of a capital, now dwindled to a provincial town, that the funeral of a popular saint might be attended by 800,000 men and 60,000 women of Baghdad and the adjacent villages.

In this City of Peace, amidst the riches of the East, the Abbassids soon disdained the abstinence and frugality of the first caliphs, and aspired to emulate the magnificence of the Persian kings.

After his wars and buildings, Al-Mansur left behind him in gold and silver about thirty millions sterling, and this treasure was exhausted in a few years by the vices or virtues of his children. His son Mahdi, in a single pilgrimage to Mecca, expended six millions of dinars in gold. A pious and charitable motive may sanctify the foundation of cisterns and caravanserais which he distributed along a measured road of 600 miles; but his train of camels, laden with snow, could serve only to astonish the natives of Arabia, and to refresh the fruits and liquors of the royal banquet.

The courtiers would surely praise the liberality of his grandson Al-Mamun, who gave away four-fifths of the income of a province, a sum of two millions four hundred thousand gold dinars, before he drew his foot from the stirrup. At the nuptials of the same prince, a thousand pearls of the largest size were showered on the head of the bride, and a lottery of lands and houses displayed the capricious bounty of fortune.

The glories of the court were brightened rather than impaired in the decline of the empire; and a Greek Ambassador might admire or pity the magnificence of the feeble Muqtadir.

'The Caliph's whole army,' says the historian Abu'l-Feda, 'both horse and foot, was under arms, which together made a body of 160,000 men. His state officers, the favourite slaves, stood near him in splendid apparel, their belts glittering with gold and gems. Near them were 7,000 eunuchs, 4,000 of them white, the remainder black. The porters or doorkeepers were in number 700. Barges and boats, with the most superb decorations, were seen swimming upon the Tigris. Nor was the palace itself less splendid, in which were hung up 38,000 pieces of tapestry, 12,500 of which were silk embroidered with gold. The carpets on the floor were twenty-two thousand. A hundred lions were brought out, with a keeper to each lion.

Among the other spectacles of rare and stupendous luxury was a tree of gold and silver spreading into eighteen large branches on which, and on the lesser boughs, sat a variety of birds made of the same precious metals, as well as the leaves of the tree. While the machinery affected spontaneous motions the several birds warbled their natural harmony.

Through this scene of magnificence the Greek ambassador was led by the Vizir to the foot of the Caliph's throne.'

* * *

What do I sing, and what does my tambourine sing?

Saying.

Take the straight path, even if it is long: marry no widow, even if she is a houri.

Proverb.

Commander of the Faithful

REGARDED as an interpolation, because it appears in the middle of a serious disucssion on esoteric matters, this extract is from *Esoteric Research* (Tahqiq-i-Batini). Reputedly written by Sir-Dan (Knower of Secrets) Daud Waraqi, an introduction to the eighteenth-century manuscript states that 'authorship identifying names can be a defilement' – so it is anonymous.

A CERTAIN caliph, wanting to test an idea on an unsophisticated person, asked his guards to range into the desert and bring him a bedouin Arab. They surrounded the first one whom they met, who happened to be a Sufi. 'The Commander of the Faithful requires your presence,' said the captain of the guard. 'Who are the faithful, and how do they come to have a Commander?' he asked. The soldiers concluded that this was indeed an unsophisticated man, and they brought him before the Caliph.

'I have been told,' said the ruler, 'that bedouins are so ignorant that they do not know the simplest things.'

'Who has told you?'

'It was during a discussion with my intellectual advisers.'

'If it is intellect that you want, the problem is easy enough. Ask me anything.'

The Caliph ordered a dish of porridge to be brought. The Arab sniffed it and began to eat. 'What is that?' asked the Caliph. 'Something that can safely be eaten,' said the bedouin. 'Yes, but what is its name?'

'Adopting the methods of formal logic, applied to the knowledge available to me, I say that this is pomegranites.'

There was a laugh from the assembled scholastics who had told the Caliph that the bedouins were fools.

'And how, pray, do you come to this conclusion?'

'By the same methods that your scholastics use. I have heard the phrase "Dates and pomegranites" used to describe tasty foods. Now I know what dates are, as I live on them. This is not dates. Therefore it must be pomegranites.'

The Ball of Marzipan

ONE day the caliph Haroun el-Raschid was conversing with a teacher. He said: 'Teacher, you know me to be a Seeker. I have all the world's goods and all the things that most men strive for. I should therefore be in the position to learn much, since I am exempted from the diversions which occupy most people.'

The teacher said: 'Everything must have a basis. You have the basis for power, for ordering men, for personal indulgence. But, when there is a lack of the essential bases, man can not only not build; like you, he very often thinks that he already possesses that basis.'

'Then teach me the basis,' said the Caliph.

'First I will teach you to understand properly the need for the basis, otherwise you will not accept the basis itself from those who know,' said the sage.

He refused to say any more because such things as he was promising are taught only when opportunity offers itself for their illustration.

It was some years before the occasion arose.

The caliph and the sage were sitting at dinner, and Haroun said: 'Sweet meats of marzipan such as these seem to me to be an excellent illustration of how human discoveries, if they are good ones, spread throughout the world, benefiting everyone.'

'O Caliph!' said the sage, 'it is now several thousand years since the invention of marzipan. Yet people are not yet universally persuaded of the excellence of marzipan. And, in addition, there are many who have never even heard of it.'

The caliph, annoyed at being so directly challenged, said to the teacher: 'I give you one day to justify that irresponsible remark. Find me someone who does not know about marzipan by tomorrow night and bring him here, or I will cast you out of my company.'

'I shall do so,' said the sage, 'because this is an opportunity for illustration, not because of your threat.'

He went into the streets of the city of Baghdad the next morning and walked about until he came across a countryman, simply dressed, holding in his hand a piece of bread, wandering as if in a daze.

The sage said to him: 'Where are you going and where are you from?'

'Take care!' said the man, 'Because I have heard of such as you — people who want to steal my bread.'

'On the contrary,' said the sage, 'I want to introduce you to something delicious, far better than bread.'

'Why would you want to do that?' asked the peasant.

'To help you know more, and to help someone else,' said the sage.

After a good deal of persuasion, the peasant was brought to the court. When he saw the guards in their resplendent costumes, the viziers and the marble fountains, he fell on his face and cried out: 'This can only be one time and one place! This is the day of resurrection, and this is the judgement-hall of God Almighty!'

'You are judging everything as best you can, but it is wrong,' said the sage, and he said much else to the man, who could only look at him with incomprehension.

When they were seated beside the Caliph, the sage explained that he had brought a man who did not know about marzipan balls.

'We shall test him,' said the Caliph. Turning to the peasant he said: 'What have you in your hand?'

'Food,' said the peasant.

The Caliph made a sign, and several balls of marzipan were brought.

'What are these?' he asked. 'They are something nutritious.'

'The wise man of our village,' said the peasant, 'always speaks of the nutrition being "dates and water and experience". I have seen dates and water, so this must be experience.'

The sage stood up.

'O Caliph! This man uses the bases of wisdom from his village to explain the things which he cannot understand without more complete explanations and experience. He has no need of marzipan. If he had, we would have to give him more information, more bases of understanding it.

'Similarly, sophisticated man likes the things, even the promise of things, which are developed from bases which are lacking or unnoticed in his surroundings.'

Ahmad Hussain and the Emperor

THE Emperor Mahmud of Ghazna was walking one day with the sage Ahmad Hussain. Ahmad had the reputation of being able to see into people's minds, and the Emperor had been trying to have him give a demonstration of his powers.

Ahmad had refused, and so Mahmud decided to try to trick him into using his special faculty.

'Ahmad,' he called.

'Yes?'

'Who do you think that man over there is?'

'He is a woodworker.'

'What would his name be?'

'Ahmad, like mine.'

'I wonder whether he has eaten anything recently.'

'Yes, something sweet.'

They called the man over, and found that these facts were correct.

'Now,' said the Emperor, 'you have refused to display your talents and are, quite worthily, concealing your spiritual gifts. Do you realise that I have forced you to demonstrate your faculty: and that people would make you into a saint if I were to repeat the story of your performance. How then would you be able to maintain your Sufi disguise of playing at being just an ordinary man?'

'I admit I can see into men's brains,' said Ahmad, 'but people never know when I am doing it. I cannot, by my nature, do it for frivolous purposes, and therefore my secret remains inviolate.'

'But you admit that you have just used those powers?'

'Not at all.'

'Then how did you know how to answer my questions correctly?'

'Easy. When you called me by name, he moved his head, so I realised that he had the same name. I inferred that he was a woodworker because, in this forest, he is looking only at trees suitable for carpentry. He has recently eaten something sweet, because he keeps brushing away bees which are attracted to his mouth.'

The King, the Sufi and the Surgeon

This tale, which is found in English in the translated Turkish Tales, as well as in the monkish collection, the Gesta Romanorum, underlines the belief that the sayings of dervish Abdals often constitute vital advice, even out of the context of the time in which they are delivered.

IN ancient times a king of Tartary was out walking with some of his noblemen. At the roadside was an *Abdal* (wandering Sufi, a 'changed one'), who cried out: 'Whoever will give me a hundred dinars, I will give him some good advice.'

The king stopped, and said: 'Abdal, what is this good advice for a hundred dinars?'

'Sir,' answered the Abdal, 'order the sum to be given to me, and I will tell it you immediately.' The king did so, expecting to hear something extraordinary.

The Dervish said to him: 'My advice is this: Never begin anything until you have reflected what will be the end of it.'

At this the nobles and everyone else present laughed, saying that the Abdal had been wise to ask for his money in advance. But the king said: 'You have no reason to laugh at the good advice this Abdal has given me. Nobody is unaware of the fact that we should think well before doing anything. But we are daily guilty of not remembering, and the consequences are evil. I very much value this Dervish's advice.'

He decided to bear the advice always in his mind, and commanded it to be written in gold on the walls and even engraved on his silver plate.

Not long afterwards a plotter desired to kill the king. He bribed the royal surgeon with a promise of the prime ministership to thrust a poisoned lancet into the king's arm. When the time came to let some of the king's blood, a silver basin was placed to catch the blood. Suddenly the surgeon became aware of the words engraved upon it: 'Never begin anything until you have reflected what will be the end of it.' It was only then that he realised that if the plotter became king he could have him killed instantly, and would not need to fulfil his bargain.

The king, seeing that the surgeon was now trembling, asked him what was wrong with him. And so he confessed the truth, at that very moment.

The plotter was seized; and the king sent for all the people who were present when the Abdal gave his advice, and said to them: 'Do you still laugh at the dervish?'

*   *   *

The power of Allah: no sound, no shape, no form. But when it manifests, none can resist it.

Proverb.

Dye your hair, certainly. But what can you do for your face?

Proverb

A Matter of Honour

A WANDERING Sufi, found in the desert, was brought to the tent of a wild Bedouin chief.

'You are a scout for our enemies, and as such we shall kill you,' said the chief.

'I am innocent,' said the Sufi.

'Do you see this sword?' asked the Sufi, drawing one; 'Before you can approach me I shall kill one of your men here. When I have done so, you will have a legitimate right to avenge his death. By so doing, I will save your honour, which is at this moment in grave danger of being sullied by shedding the blood of a harmless Sufi.'

* * *

You call me an unbeliever. I shall therefore call you a True Believer – since a lie is best met with one of similar magnitude.

Saying.

A stolen kiss is not easily returned.

Proverb.

The Pulse of the Princess

Although this tale – or at least part of it – has been called 'one of the first records of dervish psychological diagnosis and psychotherapy', and attributed to the Caliph Jafar Sadiq (died 765), teacher of Jabir and descendent of the Prophet, it appears in Rumi, and also in oral recital.

It must, however, have been well known in the Europe of the Middle Ages, because the skeleton of it appears in the chief monkish story-book, with a devout Christian moral: 'baptism is emblemed by the wife'. (Gesta Romanorum, trans. C. Swan, 1829, Tale 40, pp. 145 of Vol. I.)

SULTAN Sanjar had returned from the shrine of the Master Bahaudin in Bokhara, and ever since that he had been sad. Some people connected the two as cause and effect, but others held that the sorrow of the king was due to the mysterious illness of his daughter.

Princess Banu was wilting. Day by day her strange ailment seemed to get a stronger grip upon her. All the physicians who had been called in to advise were baffled.

Then, one day, a stranger arrived at the capital city of their country. He wore a green robe, walked bent, and called himself Shadrach the Physician. He offered to cure the princess. The King allowed him to see her, but threatened him that if he did not heal his daughter, he would be beheaded.

Surrounded by an interested audience, the physician approached the couch where the princess, wan and weary, lay. Instead of making any examination, instead of trying any remedy such as was expected of him, the green-robed man began to – tell the princess tales.

They were stories of far distant lands, of wars and heroes, of peace and of glory. And as he did so, his fingers stayed on her pulse.

At length his diagnosis was finished. The princess withdrew, and Shadrach addressed the King. 'Your Majesty, I have determined by the reactions of her pulse that she is in love. And that she is in love with someone who lives in Bokhara. That that person lives in the street of the jewellers. And that of all the men who live in the street of the jewellers in Bokhara it is none other than Abul-Fazl, a young and handsome man whom I have described to her, and at the mention of whose name she fainted. I happen to know everyone in Bokhara – as well as in many other places; and by this art I have arrived at the cause of her disease.'

Now the king wondered at the skill of this physician. He also was relieved that the cause of her illness had been discovered. And he was furiously angry because the lady was in love with such an ignoble wretch: for such Abul-Fazl was known to be.

The jeweller, however, was sent for. As soon as he arrived the princess began to recover. Within a few days she was well again, the jeweller was lording it over almost everyone, and the Physician Shadrach, as a reward, had been made Grand Vizier.

The king and the doctor realised that this insufferable youth was not for the princess. They also knew that they could not send him away, or otherwise dispose of him, because that would certainly cause the princess's malaise to return.

Shadrach provided the answer. He caused to be administered to Abdul Fazl a medicine which prematurely aged him, making him become older each day as if he had aged by twenty years. In no time at all the princess was beginning to be repulsed by his bent back and his grey locks.

At the same time Shadrach administered to himself another medicine. And by its effect, at the same pace at which the jeweller was ageing, Shadrach became younger and younger.

Before very long the princess fell in love with the young physician. When Abul-Fazl was driven from the court, the Princess Banu hardly noticed.

She and the physician and the Sultan lived happily ever after. Thus do things sometimes develop in a manner contrary to their first probability: according to what influences are brought to bear.

Maulana Dervish

MAULANA Dervish, chief of the Naqshbandi Order and one of its greatest teachers, was sitting one day in his Zavia when a furious cleric forced his way in.

'You sit there,' shouted the intruder, 'dog that you are, surrounded by disciples, obeyed by them in every particular! I, on the other hand, call men to strive towards divine mercy, through prayer and austerities, as is enjoined upon us.'

At the word 'dog', several of the Seekers rose to eject the fanatic.

'Stay,' said the Maulana, 'for "dog" is indeed a good word. I am a dog, who obeys his master – showing the sheep by signs the interpretation of our Master's desires. Like a dog I infuriate the interloper and the thief. And I wag my tail in pleasure when my master's Friends come near.'

'Just as barking and wagging and love are attributes of the dog, we exercise them: for our Master has us, and does not do his own barking and wagging.'

* * *

The harshness of a teacher is better than the reputed softness of the parent.

Proverb.

Hit your hand on a stone and expect it to hurt.

Proverb.

Self-Deception

As long as you ask the question you think that should be answered for you, without taking heed of my assurance that you are in greater need of certain other instruction – so long will I be unable to help you and so long will you believe that I am no use to you.

But you, in ignorance of the instruction which you need, will inevitably conclude that there is some other reason for our not being in concert and harmony. You invent the reason – and your self-esteem makes it 'true' for you.

(*Sheikh Mir Khan*).

*   *   *

Life: sometimes the man on the saddle, sometimes the saddle on the man.

Proverb.

It will pass, whatever it is.

Proverb.

The Camel and the Tent

*This tale is handed down from the Sufi Sheikh, Abdul-Aziz
of Mecca, who died in the seventh century. He is said to have
been given the 'elixir of life' by Mohammed, whose companion
he was, and to be still alive, in one sense or another,
nourished by this magical potion.*

*Other versions say that the 'potion' was in fact an
exercise called 'imprisoning the breath', which – although
dangerous for those who do not know how to use it – enables
one to put the body into a state of suspended animation.*

*The method is used by the followers of several Sufi Orders;
though Abdul-Aziz's affiliation was with the Qalandari
(whom some say he founded) and the Chishtis.*

A BEDOUIN, making a long desert trek, pitched his small black
tent and lay down to sleep. As the night grew colder his camel
woke him up with a nudge. 'Master, it is cold. May I put my nose
inside the tent to warm it?' The traveller agreed, and settled down
to sleep again. Scarcely an hour had passed, however, before the
camel began to feel colder. 'Master, it is much colder. Can I put
my head inside the tent?'

First his head was admitted to the tent, then, on the same
argument, his neck. Finally, without asking, the camel heaved his
whole bulk under the cloth. When he had, as he thought, settled
himself, the bedouin was lying beside the camel, with no covering
at all. The camel had uprooted the tent, which hung, totally
inadequately, across his hump.

Where has the tent gone?' asked the confused camel.

The Curse

A PRETENDED Sufi took some wheat to a mill to be ground into flour.

'Grind it now, and make haste about it,' he said, for these charlatans are always trying to make people do things for them.

'I have no time,' said the miller.

'If you do not,' said the rogue, 'I shall curse your mill.'

'I would like to see you do that,' said the miller, himself a real Sufi, 'because if you could get things done by such methods you would not be here trying to make me grind your wheat.'

*　*　*

The happiness of the superficial: when a man who has lost his donkey finds it again.

Proverb.

My leg is not lame, Allah's earth is not small.

Proverb.

Pleasant and Unpleasant

PEOPLE say that they want help, when they want attention.

They say that they want to listen, when they want to be heard.

We know this by what you say, by how you look, by what we can feel.

Everyone else would feel it, too, if they were not similarly self-absorbed and uninterested in you.

You must first of all find out from yourself if you want to learn and why you want to learn.

If you go somewhere to buy something, you must first earn the money, and have some idea of what you need.

If you just have idle wants and do not know your needs, you have a long way to go.

If you become diverted from us by our behaviour, you would never have been able to keep pace with us, anyway.

If this sounds unpleasant, it does not signify that it is meant to be unpleasant. If you think that we are unpleasant, you are holding up a mirror to yourself, and saying. 'Look at them!'

(*Salahudin Afranji*).

*　　*　　*

Because sugar is not arsenic, many graves are full.

Proverb.

Khwaja Ahrar

THE miracles of the Master Ahrar were of such daily occurrence that some people said: 'What else do you expect? He is a Changed One – such things are nothing to him. To heal, to prolong life, to know all, to be in two places at once: these are marks of sainthood.'

But those who were amazed by wonders took pleasure in them, feeling blessed and self-righteous. They craved still more marvels.

One of these, Rustem Kashgari, said: 'Master of the Great Work! The All-Highest has indeed bestowed upon the Order (Tariqa) a magnanimous endowment, that we shall be both benefited and reassured of your celestial mandate: and can thus in sure faith travel the Way.'

The Khwaja said: 'Friend, this is not faith. I assure you that there are on this earth at any one time at least forty thousand celestial visitants in the form of men. Each one may seem to you to be just an ordinary man. Yet each one makes unknown miracles happen every day. Because these wonders are for a purpose and not for delighting the eyes of men, these hidden ones are generally unknown and hence almost always uncelebrated. They may even be shunned.

Even when they are those who talk of spirituality, they may be among those who are forbidden to perform evidentiary miracles, lest they impress the sensation-seeking self-esteem of the populace.

The man converted by being witness to a miracle is less than equal to a lowly dog on the Way. His belief is due only to a form of excitement, which people miscall faith. If you are sincere, you will perceive the quality of real men directly and instantly, and not through miracles and tales of miracles. When you can feel this essence, this jewel, in those whom others take to be an ordinary man, or take to be the Master, call yourself a Traveller on the Way.'

(*Ahrar-Nama*)

Saadi: On Envy

You cannot, however you may try, stop the mouths of critics.

If a man prefers privacy, and does not seek the company of others: they attack him, saying that such a one flees like a demon.

If he laughs, they cannot believe that he is at all sober.

The rich man cannot hide from them, for he is described by them as a 'wordly Pharaoh'.

If a dervish is in difficulties, they say that it is due to his being evil and having ill-luck.

When a prosperous man has troubles, they hold that it is a blessing and a sign of the intervention of God.

They say: 'How long can prominence abide? Is happiness not always followed by misfortune?'

And when they find that a poor man attains success and felicity – they grind their teeth in envy, carping: 'The world cherishes only the useless!'

When your hands are fully occupied by work you are 'greedy'; but just stop working and you are a 'real beggar'.

If you speak, you are a 'rattling drum'. If you remain silent, you are 'nothing more than a picture on a wall'.

The forebearing person is, to them, no man at all; for, 'Poor thing, he cannot even raise his head because of fear!' But let them come upon a brave and mettlesome man, and they will scuttle from him, whining: 'What kind of a madman is this?'

The man who eats very little is, to them, a miser, hoarding up his substance. If his food is delicious and fine, though, 'He is a slave to his stomach and a worshipper of the flesh'.

An unceremonious rich man, wearing simple clothes: they slash with tongues like blades, for: 'Odious one, he has money sure enough, yet grudges to spend it even on himself!'

Now let him wear good clothes and arrange a pleasant hall:

They will drive him out of his wits, claiming that he is without a doubt effeminate.

If a devout man has not travelled, the migrants among them

will call him 'A man who has not journeyed an arm's-length from his wife's side.' How could *he* possibly have any knowledge, art or skill?

But they will flay the wanderer, too:

'Fortune has passed him by, for if any luck at all had been his, he would not have had to roam like that from town to town.'

(*Sheikh Saadi of Shiraz*).

* * *

I ask about the sky, but the answer is about a rope.

Proverb.

A yellow dog is brother to the jackal.

Proverb.

Hazrat Bahaudin Naqshband

ONE said:

'What shall I do to be answered?'

El Shah answered:

'You shall avoid those who imagine themselves to be the People of Salvation. They think that they are saved, or that they have the means to save. In reality, they are all but lost.

'These are the people, like today's Magians, Jews and Christians, who recite dramatic tales, threaten and cajole many times in succession with the same admonitions, they cry out that you must become committed to their creed.

'The result of this is an imitation, a sentimentalist. Anyone can be "given" this spurious type of belief, and can be made to feel that it is real faith.

'But this is not the original Way of Zoroaster, of Moses, of Jesus. It is the method discovered by desperate men for the inclusion in their ranks of large numbers. Far from being saved or made complete, such enthusiasts are set aside in a trained band for eventual dissolution: like a cloud which for a time seems to have substance, but which a puff of wind will banish to nothingness.

'But do not enter into controversy with them. They have been deceived to take the false for the true, because they preferred the easier to the harder test. They would see even an angel as the devil himself.

'It is always thus with the weak inheritors of the Real Ones. Just as lazy sons live off an orchard which their father tended, thinking themselves clever, righteous and rightful owners, until – unpruned – it starts to fail.

'You will be answered if you seek the man who will refuse the easy method of preaching and practise as I have outlined it: a method suitable only for the breaking of horses and causing attachment to one's person, or the production of ignorant and helpless slaves.'

Prayer

ONE man went to see another, asking his help in some matter. The visitor was astonished and then infuriated when the other, supposedly pious, said:

'I cannot help you. I have to say my prayers.'

He swore at the man and later reported this incident to Bahaudin Naqshband.

Bahaudin said:

'We have here the illustration of a defect in thought. It is being assumed that the prayerful man was a hypocrite, since it has been said, 'The best prayer is useful action.'

'But there are two possible situations here: that of the hypocrite and that of the wise man.

'All will depend upon the inner capabilities and true state of the prayerful man.

'If the prayerful man is greedy and interested only in his own salvation, he will speak the words which have been reported.

'If, on the other hand, the prayerful man is illuminated, and knows that his prayer is more useful than any action which he could take, he will also speak exactly the same words as have been reported.

'Yet, although the same words have been spoken, the applicant, ignorant that one set of words can cover two distinct sets of circumstances, may instantly interpret things to the discredit of the prayerful man.

'In so doing he is either reacting from ignorance, in which he thinks that he is ill-treated because he does not know better; or he may be judging everything by a critical cast of mind which generally tends to be so shallow that it will interpret speech as an attack.

'In this case, short of the immediate perception of what the real situation was at the time, it is not possible to declare whether the prayerful man was the lowest or the highest of individuals: whether, in fact, he was ruining himself by engaging in a prayer rather than help, concentrating his own greed; or whether, gifted with a certain insight, he was proceeding along the road to truth.

'It has been said that the critic is one who judges others by himself.

'If the applicant had been an enlightened man, he would have been able to see the true situation. Then he would have remonstrated with the prayerful man, and helped him through his own insight, if that man were in the wrong. If he were in the right, he would have approached him in a different way.

'To come to me to seek approbation or interpretation is useful only if the applicant can realise that he can best be served not by legal judgement but by learning from this that his best of all procedures would be to place himself on the path to gain inner cognition.

'Failing that, he must learn that it exists. This information alone gives him a chance of avoiding irrational action.'

(*Naqsh-i-Naqshband*).

* * *

Have the nature of a dervish: *then* wear a stylish cap.
Saying.

Pick up a bee from kindness, and learn the limitations of kindness.
Proverb.

The Horseman in a Hurry

ONCE upon a time there was a man who was asleep and who swallowed a venomous creature, which stuck in his throat.

He got up in a sort of delirium and started to cough and shake himself, to try to get rid of the affliction, which he did not fully understand.

At that moment a man on a horse, happening by, saw at a glance what had happened.

He immediately raised his whip and started to beat the man black and blue, raining down upon him blows without mercy.

The half-crazed patient tried to cry out to him to stop, but could not get the words out. As he ran, or writhed on the ground, or rolled over, he found that he was always sustaining a hail of pitiless blows.

The horseman said not a word.

Eventually, with a mighty heave, the poisonous animal was thrown up by the protesting stomach of the afflicted man.

It fell to the ground and slithered away.

The horseman, without a word, spurred his beast and rode away.

Only then did the other man realise that what seemed to him an unjustified assault in his misery had, in fact, been the only way in which he could be rid of the creature before the venom were injected into his system.

*　　*　　*

Much travel is needed before the raw man is ripened.

Proverb.

Class and Nation

DIFFERENT sections of the community are, to all realities, 'nations'.

Beware of people who ask you questions, when they already have opinions which they want to have confirmed, or by means of which they propose, unknowingly, to reject you and thus support their own conclusions.

Association with such people is not only fruitless: it is the mark of an ignorant man.

The clerics, doctors, literary men, nobles and peasants, really could be called nations; for each one has its own customs and casts of thought. To imagine that they are just the same as you simply because they live in the same country or speak the same language is a feeling to be examined. All enlightened people eventually reject this assumption.

(*Samarqandi*).

* * *

Patience is bitter, but bears a sweet fruit.

Proverb.

Be kind to the hawk and harm the sparrow.

Proverb.

Letters

ᴄᴅ

THE ordinary man writes a letter with little thought for the state of the person who reads it; and much regard for his own state.

The thoughtful man writes a letter bearing in mind what he thinks will be the mind of the person who reads it.

The learned man writes few letters, in case he cannot anticipate the state of the recipient.

The Sufi writes no letter until he can know exactly what will be the state of mind in the man when he receives it.

The Adept writes any letter which has to be written.

The Arif (gnostic) has no need of writing nor receiving letters. But such is the confusion of mankind that:

If the Arif does not write, he will be thought very great or perhaps very heedless. The Adept, writing a necessary letter, will be judged as if he was an emotionalist or propagandist. The Sufi, divining the state of mind of the recipient, will be thought to write unsuitable letters. The learned man will be thought, from his paucity of letters, to be more occupied in something else. The thoughtful man will not be able to communicate well, in case something he writes gives offence. The ordinary man, writing all kinds of letters, may have them collected and selected. If he writes enough, people will choose those which seem to them valuable. On the basis of these, he can be erroneously styled a saint.

(*Shah Hasan*).

*   *   *

One day the cub will become a wolf, even if it has been reared among the sons of man.

Proverb.

The Voice

THE voice of the supreme leadership of higher knowledge is always there. It is not heard by ordinary people because their personal or group vanity makes them deaf. As a consequence they say that it is not audible: or, worse, they listen to another voice or voices, which their vanity, again, makes them feel is the true one.

There is so much that can feed personal vanity admixed with moral teachings commonly accepted as 'good' or 'true' ones that even the most faithful followers of these are indulging their vanity just as surely as the trained or self-appointed critic is, in reality, exercising his vanity in his criticising, not learning, teaching nor contributing to anything.

The voice, always speaking, is saying: 'You cannot struggle against or avoid vanity until you know where it is operating.' By displacement, people attach their vanity to institutions and try to make them endure long enough after they have any use.

(*Mohammed Ali-Shah*).

* * *

Better the demon which makes you improve than the angel who threatens.

Proverb.

The sort of man who, throwing a stone upon the ground, would miss.

Proverb.

The Four Men and the Interpreter

This allegory of Rumi's has been used since the thirteenth century to characterise both the different 'languages' of men – their wanting the same thing and thinking it is different – and the 'four men' who are said to battle within the hearts of every individual.

It is from the Mathnavi, the Couplets of Inner Meaning, *which Rumi left behind, and which has been called 'The Koran in Persian'.*

FOUR people were given a piece of money.

The first was a Persian. He said: 'I will buy with this some *Angur.*'

The second was an Arab. He said: 'No, because *I* want *Inab.*'

The third was a Turk. He said: 'I do not want *Inab*, I want *Uzüm.*'

The fourth was a Greek. He said: '*I* want *Stafil.*'

Because they did not know what lay behind the names of things, these four started to fight. They had information but no knowledge.

One man of wisdom present could have reconciled them all, saying: 'I can fulfil the needs of all of you, with one and the same piece of money. If you honestly give me your trust, your one coin will become as four; and four at odds will become as one united.'

Such a man would know that each in his own language wanted the same thing, grapes.

* * *

Each flies with its own kind: pigeon with pigeon, hawk with hawk.

Proverb.

The Sultans and the Taxpayer

WHILE legal redress of hurt to the mind is always hard to find, there is an anonymous way which many of the successful rulers in our time and in times of old practised. It was carried out, and still is, in some places, by the instruction of the Men of Wisdom who never appear in public, but whom the rulers heed. It is called the 'Matter of Pruning'.

Officials of every grade – shall we take tax-collectors – are subject to no control save the rules and regulations and the need to appear satisfactory to immediate superiors.

As a result there are as many abuses of stupidity as of corruption. In any society the corruption of the heart is as harmful as that of the pocket.

Enlightened administrations employ people who visit these tax-collectors and others, supposedly as taxpayers. If they are treated heartlessly or stupidly, they report this to the department whose concern is such matters, and the offenders are 'pruned': that is to say, they are sent to some place where their defects cannot harm others.

There are many stories of this: how justice was meted out by Haroun and his Vizier, visiting people in disguise. Know, therefore, that 'Haroun' means the body of people dedicated to justice, and Haroun and the Vizier are the means, in the healthy society, whereby the 'pruning' is carried out.

Where there is no such pruning, the country is in a state of disaster, whether it knows it or not, and whether there is a public fuss to assuage the conscience or not. There must always be this pruning.

(*Mohsin Ardabili*).

The Thief

A MAN of Merv, well known as the home of complicated thinkers, ran shouting one night through the city's streets. 'Thief, Thief!' he cried.

The people surrounded him, and when he was a little calmer, asked: 'Where was the thief?'

'In my house.'

'Did you see him?'

'No.'

'Was anything missing?'

'No.'

'How do you know there was a thief then?'

'I was lying in bed when I remembered that thieves break into houses without a sound, and move very quietly. I could hear nothing, so I knew that there was a thief in the house, you fool!'

(*Niamat Khan*).

*   *   *

Know your measure.
                    Proverb.

What is their opinion in their cups, those who have said that wine is an abomination?
                    Proverb.

Seeing Double

A FATHER said to his double-seeing son:
  'Son, you see two instead of one.'
  'How can that be?' the boy replied. 'If I were, there would seem to be *four* moons up there in place of two.'

(*Hakim Sanai of Ghazna*).

* * *

If you want to be a calligrapher, write, and write, and write.

Proverb.

The liar has a bad memory.

Proverb.

Why ?

A MAN said to a Dervish: 'Why do I not see you more often?'
The Dervish replied: 'Because the words "Why have you not been to see me?" are sweeter to my ear than the words "Why have you come again?".'

(*Mulla Jami*).

* * *

Tomorrow there will be apricots.

Proverb.

If the father cannot, the son will finish the task.

Proverb.

Yusuf, Son of Husain

DESIRING to become a disciple, Yusuf sought out Dhun'Nun, and acted as a servant to him for a year.

After this period, Dhun'Nun asked:

'What do you want of me?'

Yusuf said: 'Permission to serve for another year.'

After the second year, Dhun'Nun said: 'Ask something of me.'

Yusuf said: 'Tell me the Most Great Name.'

Dhun'Nun did not answer, and Yusuf continued as his servant.

One day, Dhun'Nun handed Yusuf a dish, covered with a cloth. He said: 'Take this to the dervish who lives on the other side of this river. Do not remove the cloth under any circumstances.'

Yusuf said: 'By my head and heart, it shall be so.'

Dhun'Nun said: 'If it is so, the dervish will tell you the Great Name.'

But as he was crossing the river, he became curious as to what might be in the dish, and he untied the cloth. A rat leapt out, fell into the Nile and was carried away.

When he reached the place of the dervish, Yusuf gave him the bowl, and said, 'Tell me the Great Name.'

The dervish said: 'You could not bear a rat in a bowl: can you therefore protect the Great Name? You have failed your test.'

He returned to the Master, very depressed in spirits.

Dhun'Nun sent him to his own country, saying, 'In due course you will receive your initiation.'

It was fifty years before Yusuf, because of this and other heedlessnesses, attained discipline enough to learn and keep the Great Name.

(*Attar*).

Why the Dervish Hides Himself

꧁꧂꧁꧂꧁꧂꧁꧂꧁꧂꧁꧂꧁꧂꧁꧂꧁꧂꧁꧂꧁꧂꧁꧂꧁꧂

RUMI was asked by his son:

'Why is the dervish hidden? Is this a self-concealment: done by means of clothing? Is there something within him which he disguises?'

The Master said: 'It might be in any way. Some write love-poems, and people think that they mean ordinary love. The calling sometimes conceals the real position in the Way: there are traders, like Baba Farid; some write literature. Others pursue other external activities.

'This may be done for defence against worldly people. Some deliberately act in a way which society might disapprove, to gain peace. The Prophet has therefore said: "God has hidden the Men of Greatest Knowledge."

'Any strategem may be adopted by the Followers of the Way to gain peace when they might otherwise be hindered.'

The Master then recited:

Ever-knowing, as they hide they seek.

To the ordinary man, they appear other than they are.

In inward light they roam: making miracles come to pass.

– Yet none knows who they are.

(Aflaki: Munaqib el-Arifin).

* * *

For every Pharoah there is a Moses.

Proverb.

The Dog and the Dervishes

A PARTY of dervishes, accompanied by some pupils, stopped on their journey to have a picnic.

They spread a cloth by the roadside and put large stones on its corners, so that the wind would not disturb it.

Noticing their preparations, a stray dog began to nose around.

One of the disciples said: 'We are going to have difficulty with that dog. Giving it scraps will only encourage it to wreck our meal.'

One of the Dervishes replied: 'Action is superior to intellection. Stop thinking that, and continue to place stones on the corners of the cloth.'

The dog made the rounds of all the stones, sniffing them, and then he ran away, barking.

One of the Dervishes, who was reputed to know the language of animals, said:

'He is saying: "If these people only put out stones for their own meal, what hope have I of scraps of real food from them?".'

* * *

Your magic talisman is powerful: but are you a Solomon to make it work?

Proverb.

Be *in* the world, but not *of* the world.

Proverb.

The Prayer and the Curse of the Dervish

This tradition of the Naqshbandi Order is from the venerated manuscript Asrar-i-Khajagan *(Secrets of the Masters), where it is attributed to the Sheikh Munawwar Shah who died in 1848. His shrine is at Lahore.*

The tale echoes the tradition that certain people – especially Sufis of a certain rank and some descendents of Mohammed – may curse a person in order to give him a blessing.

MAN, because of his selfishness, does not know that prayer often 'goes by contraries'.

There was once a dervish whose vocation was powerful, though he suffered from lapses of aspiration; sometimes he wished for things for himself which he did not deserve.

One day he was climbing a steep hill and because he was tired he prayed that he might have help in the effort. Immediately – as from nowhere – a man appeared and forced the dervish to take him on his back.

It happened that a woman was coming down the hill at the same time, with her child in her arms. Seeing a venerable figure, himself almost unable to make the ascent, performing what she took to be such a self-sacrificing act as to carry a companion on his back, she stopped to ask a favour.

'O dervish! Bless this child of mine!'

Remembering this time the working of contraries, the dervish called out:

'May the child be cursed!'

Whereupon the unhappy woman burst into tears.

And even the villain whom the dervish was carrying was so incensed by his seeming heartlessness that he beat him soundly and went on his way alone.

Encounter with the Devil

A CERTAIN devout man, convinced that he was a sincere Seeker after Truth, embarked upon a long course of discipline and study.

He had many experiences, under various teachers both in his inner and outer life, over a considerable period of time.

One day he was meditating when he suddenly saw the Devil sitting beside him.

'Away, demon!' he cried, 'for you have no power to harm me; I am treading the Path of the Elect.'

The apparition disappeared.

A truly wise man passing by told him, sadly:

'Alas, my friend, you have grafted effort upon such an unsure basis as your unaltered fear, greed, and self-esteem that you have arrived at your ultimate possible experience.'

'How so?' asked the Seeker.

'That "devil" is, in reality, an angel. "Devil" is only how *you* saw him.'

* * *

Brave is the thief who carries a lamp in his hand.

Proverb.

The Beard of the Dervish

Sayed Khidr Rumi (died 1360), who is reputed to have made teaching journeys to England and China in the fourteenth century, is credited with having used this story to illustrate (1) just because a man may know what he should not do, he does not necessarily know what he should do; (2) people assume that one thing (liking your beard) is the opposite of another (plucking out your beard). This version is from Attar's Parliament of the Birds, *written in the thirteenth century.*

A CERTAIN dervish had a venerable beard, of which he was very proud. He passed a great deal of his time in devotional exercises but some of his attention was upon the beard, the mark of his gravity.

Moses was on his way to Sinai, when the dervish stopped him. He said: 'Please ask God for me why it is that although I am devout and unceasing in my religious duties, I never arrive at a spiritual fulfilment.'

Moses agreed to do so, and God replied to him: 'It is true that this dervish is a seeker, but his thoughts are often of his beard.'

When Moses returned from his communion and related the message, the dervish was struck by conscience. Now he spent a large part of his time plucking out his wonderful beard, hair by hair, and reproaching himself for having considered it as something of importance.

Now when Gabriel visited Moses, he said to him, talking of this dervish: 'At one time he thought too much about the beauty of his beard. Now he is thinking about his beard just as much, even more, in fact.'

The Ants and the Pen

This allegory, based upon an argument of Rumi's (Mathnavi, IV) was used by the teacher Saad el-Din Jabravi, the founder of the Saadi Sufi School.

The intention in this version is to admit the usefulness of the scientific ('ant') method of investigation, while insisting that another kind of knowledge ('literacy') not normally associated with man, must be acquired in order to make sense of life.

Jabravi died in Damascus in 1335. His tales are still current, accompanied by the argument that allegory is essential to the human mind to envisage ideas which cannot be captured by any other method.

AN ant one day strayed across a piece of paper and saw a pen writing in fine, black strokes.

'How wonderful this is!' said the ant. 'This remarkable thing, with a life of its own, makes squiggles on this beautiful surface, to such an extent and with such energy that it is equal to the efforts of all the ants in the world. And the squiggles which it makes! These resemble ants: not one, but millions, all run together.'

He repeated his ideas to another ant, who was equally interested. He praised the powers of observation and reflection of the first ant.

But another ant said: 'Profiting, it must be admitted, by your efforts, I have observed this strange object. But I have determined that it is not the master of this work. You failed to notice that this pen is attached to certain other objects, which surround it and drive it on its way. These should be considered as the moving factor, and given the credit.' Thus were fingers discovered by the ants.

But another ant, after a long time, climbed over the fingers and realised that they comprised a hand, which he thoroughly explored, after the manner of ants, by scrambling all over it.

He returned to his fellows: 'Ants!' he cried, 'I have news of importance for you. Those smaller objects are a part of a large one. It is this which gives motion to them.'

But then it was discovered that the hand was attached to an arm, and the arm to a body, and that there were two hands, and that there were feet which did no writing.

The investigations continue. Of the mechanics of the writing, the ants have a fair idea. Of the meaning and intention of the writing, and how it is ultimately controlled, they will not find out by their customary method of investigation. Because they are 'literate'.

*　　*　　*

The reading of the ignorant: like a donkey eating a melon which it has stamped into the mire.

Proverb.

When the hawk said that he was simply resting on a ruin, the owls who lived there cried out: 'He lies! He is trying to steal our home by guile.'

Proverb.

Who Recognised the Master

Sufis frequently point out that the respect given to authority figures is often the product of sentiment, publicity or mal-observation. Hilali, the sixteenth-century teacher of Samar-kand, used to illustrate this doctrine by direct demonstration.

This series of planned incidents is from Salik's Tibb-el-Arif (Medicine of the Gnostic).

HILALI, accompanied by five of his disciples, went on a long journey through Central Asia. From time to time Hilali made his companions act in various ways. These are some of their adventures:

When they reached Balkh and a deputation of the great people from the city came out to greet the Master, Hilali said to Yusuf Lang: 'Be thou the Master.' Yusuf was received and honoured. Reports spread of the miracles which he had accomplished merely by staying under the same roof as certain sick people. 'This is what people think Dervishhood is, and what we know it is not,' said Hilali.

In Surkhab the companions entered the town all dressed the same, none walking in front of another. 'Which is the Great Master?' asked the chief of the town. 'I am he,' said Hilali. Immediately the people fell back exclaiming, 'We knew it by the Light in his Eyes.'

'Take a lesson from this,' said Hilali to his companions.

When the company entered Qandahar they were given a feast by the Chief Sardar, all sitting in a circle. Hilali had given orders that he was to be treated as the least of the disciples, and that Jafar Akhundzada was to be treated as the Master. But the Chief Sardar said: 'Verily this least of the companions shines with the inner light, and whatever you may say of him, I regard him as the Magnetic Centre of the Age.'

All saluted Hilali, who was forced to recognise that the Sardar, although a ruler, had also the capacity to perceive what men do not perceive.

Solomon, the Mosquito and the Wind

‍ꙮꙮꙮ

This famous tale of Central Asia is often used as a demonstration of the Sufi teaching that justice is only relative, though man claims that it is absolute.

On a famous occasion, challenged by an Armenian philosopher to 'prove' that fables were intended for anything more than entertainment or the inculcation of simple morals, the Sufi wanderer Kazi Naim told this tale, in the eighteenth century.

He claimed that when one could see the limitations of personal vanity, a 'different world' might become perceptible. This assertion was, however, not accepted by those present, and Naim was actually tried for 'robbing the people of entertainment', sentenced to be handed to the justice of the mob in Astrakhan. He was stoned to death, saying, 'You are doing useful work, for violence may impress truth on life in spite of intentions.'

The story is also found in Rumi's Mathnavi.

ONE day a mosquito went to the court of King Solomon the Wise.

'O great Solomon, upon thee Peace,' he cried, 'I come to seek redress at your Court for the injustices which are daily being performed against me.'

Solomon said: 'State your complaint, and it will certainly be heard.'

Said the mosquito: 'Illustrious and all-just one, my complaint is against the Wind. Whenever I go out into the open, the Wind comes along and blows me away. I therefore have no hope of reaching the places which I regard as my lawful destination.'

King Solomon spoke: 'In accordance with the accepted principles of justice, no complaint can be accepted unless the other party is present to answer the charge.'

He turned to his courtiers and commanded: 'Call the Wind to make out his own case.'

The Wind was called up, and presently the breeze which heralded his coming was felt to rustle slowly, then stronger.

And the mosquito shouted: 'O Great King! I withdraw my complaint, because the air is driving me round and round in circles, and before the Wind is actually here I shall have been swept away.'

Thus were the circumstances imposed both by the plaintiff and the court found to be impossible to the cause of justice.

*   *   *

The definition of the word 'finished' is: 'This word means *finished*.'

Proverb.

The Bees and the Hollow Tree

This is a favourite tale of Balkan dervishes. It is attributed to Sayed Jafar (died 1598 in Ephesus) who was a successor of Ibrahim Gulshani of Cairo, who founded the Gulshani Order, a combination of the Four Paths of Sufism. He died in 1553.

Jafar is popularly believed to have 'visited the stars', as a sort of precursor to today's spacemen, in a luminous chariot without perceptible motive-power. The Gulshanis handed back their metaphysical endowment 'in a brass, silver and copper casket' to the Azamia ('Greater') Brethren in the seventeenth century, retaining, it is said, only the powers of obtaining interviews with certain historical figures long dead.

SAYED Jafar, Grand Master of the Four Paths, was asked by an enquirer:

'Which of the Paths is the best of Paths, and why is it that there are so many bodies of earnest people surrounding institutions teaching enlightenment?'

He answered:

'Once upon a time there was a forest, which sprouted from seedlings, which grew into trees. These trees lived until their appointed time, giving fruit, shelter and a livelihood to many creatures. Then, for a good reason, their task completed, the trees died, and the forest became lifeless. Lifeless, that is, except for a number of bees, which were looking for a home, and looking for a place to build up corporate life. They found that many of the dead trees were hollow, and in them they built their hives.

'The trees served well enough for many generations of bees. Then, one by one, in the normal course of decay, the trunks began to fall. Those bees who were still in solid enough trees pointed to their less fortunate fellows, saying:

' "Look how wicked they are! This is a punishment for them." Others said, about them and others:

' "Let us bring them to our hives for they are destitute and should be helped. This might have happened to us, after all."

Yet others said : "How useless were their hives, that they collapsed like that. Let us take care that ours do not follow."

'But, in spite of what they said, little by little, the trees all fell, and all the bees were rendered homeless, at different times.

'The bees thought about things in an obvious way. Many of them did not realise that the hives were deliberately made just for shelter and providing honey. Many did not realise that they should have taken advantage of the trees and hastened their work before they collapsed. This last difficulty was because bees did not trouble to set aside a part of their time and effort to study the nature of their environment.'

* * *

Nothing cheap without reason.

Proverb.

The Effects—and Use—of Music

Many of the dervish teachers have forbidden the use of music: not because they regard it as of no value, but because they regard it 'As of such fundamental value that to listen to it wrongly provides pleasure and prevents its function in a means to Truth'. (Ibn Darani)

It is, however, difficult for the cultivated man to believe that his perception of music is 'In fact the lowest range of the sublime possibilities of music'. (Hatim el-Askari)

Saadi builds these ideas into a memorable autobiographical fragment in his Manners of Dervishes.

ALTHOUGH my revered mentor Sheikh Abu-el-Faraj Shamsudin, son of Jauzi (the Peace of God upon him!) used to advise me to abandon my liking for song and take up solitary contemplation, I was young and full of appreciation of it.

I followed a path, therefore, at variance with the commands of my master and enjoyed music and song in the company of dervishes. And whenever on those occasions, I remembered the Sheikh's admonition, I used to say:

'If an abstainer were to taste wine
He would excuse even the intoxicated.'

One night, however, I came upon a number of people gathered around a singer. His voice was worse than hearing the news of one's father's death. Sometimes the fingers of the audience were in their ears, sometimes on their lips, trying to hush him. Nobody was pleased except when they got up to go. I said to my host: 'Give me cotton wool, for God's sake, for my ears: or show me the door.'

But out of regard for the group I remained where I was.

When morning dawned, I took off my turban and placed it, together with a gold piece and my thanks, before the singer. My friends were surprised and amused. One said:

'In this action you have not been guided by wisdom. Presenting the turban of a man of culture, and a piece of gold to a man who has never been given anything!'

I answered: 'Cease your reproaches, for the remarkable qualities of this man have become visible to me.'

'Tell me his qualities,' said my friend, 'so that I may befriend him and earn forgiveness.'

I told him: 'My revered master has repeatedly told me to give up music and song. I have until now ignored his advice. Through the performance of this singer I have been able to realise the adverse possibilities of music.'

* * *

Haste is from the Devil.

Proverb.

Confessions of John of Antioch

*Reputed to have lived in the thirteenth century, Yahya (John)
of Antioch lived, worked and travelled in Syria, Palestine,
Egypt and India. He may also have visited Central Asia.
Though well known in oral tradition for his ' Sayings', very
few written records of his life survive. They have never been
collected.*

QUITE early in my youth I noticed, provoked by what I do not
know, that the beliefs and the loves and hatreds of people seemed
to originate with the teachings of their parents and the community
to which they belonged. The Mandeans, for instance, hated the
Christians, although they knew little about them, and did not want
to increase their knowledge. And the Christians believed pre-
posterous things about the Moslems, in spite of living amongst
them and having a daily refutation of their prejudices, which they
were unprepared to accept. Again, philosophers debated doctrines
and arrived at answers which were profoundly affected by the
quantity and nature of the knowledge with which they started
their exercises, and their pre-judgements about the world, life and
people.

I was for these reasons attracted to the people of the Sufi
thought, although, aware that I was myself greatly affected
by changes in mood, in speculation which was a mental habit
with me, and by hope and fear I doubted whether I could reach
the understanding of humanity which these marvellous people
exhibited.

At first, because of these shortcomings, I found myself attracted
by the assurance which came, as I saw, to many, by the repeated
affirmation by teachers of all kinds that their own path, and theirs
alone, led to salvation. I saw that it did, indeed, lead to a stilling
of the searching and uncertainties of life. Again, because of the
same reasons, as I soon realised, I was at one time powerfully
moved by the expedient devised by the Hindus, which consisted

189

mainly in removing oneself, by an effort of the will, from the need to dwell upon human problems at all.

At length, I became a follower of the Sufis, because in my intercourse with them I discovered that they invariably helped protect me from the consequences of my selfishness, and seemed to help grow in me that part which could assent to the need to regard my fellow man as my brother, and my brother as myself. All religions preserved, it seemed to me, the indications, in the form of aphorisms, of what should be attempted. None of them preserved the means by which a man could make his way from where he received the message up to the point where he practised the message and became whole.

I understood, long after I first started to follow the Sufi people, that entry into the body of the Sufis is possible in truth only after one has passed beyond the 'entry with the tongue' and the 'entry with the heart' alike.

The Sufis, by accepting and passing on the capacity of guides in this way, this way between where man finds himself to be and where he wants to be, made themselves knowing mediums fully sensitised, so that a certain high power could move through them.

They did this only at the risk of loss of personal repute, (for men did not understand them) and by shunning the customary attachments of the world until they could truly resist them (and thereby often foreswore the great dignities which they could otherwise have had), and they also took as their watchword the most courageous contract: 'We can help you to help yourself, and we must discharge our duty setting aside whether we are understood by the generality of people, and our help to you is at whatever cost to our potential achievements in the superficial world.'

These are the men who love man, and whose love enables him to find the road to his own home.

Silent Teaching

THE Great Master Ahmad Yasavi of Khorasan spent nine years in irregular and strange contact with certain of his disciples. They were Shabaz, Lukman, Jalal and Jan-Nush. During this time he gave them practically no verbal instruction, and performed no rituals, studied no books.

Instead, he had them observe him and practise applied arts, which included carpet-weaving and building and sometimes their own professions. In the city of Balkh he sometimes called them to him to see some object which he had to show them. For other studies he sent them to listen to apparently irrelevant expositions given by others.

It was by his inner powers that all these experiences became transformed within the consciousness of these followers. This is the process known as 'teaching by signs'. At times these four cried: 'Why cannot we attend the exercise-meetings of the Master?'

And yet it is they who became masters, the founders of Orders, and reached in the end the High Attainment of the Aim.

May their innermost consciousness be sanctified.

Jangju Khanabadi: *Isharat-i-Khwajagan:* (Signs of the Masters). Ahmad Yasavi died in 1166.

Three Things

THREE things cannot be retrieved:
The arrow once sped from the bow
The word spoken in haste
The missed opportunity.

(Ali the Lion, Caliph of Islam, son-in-Law of Mohammed the Prophet).

Table Talk
by Idries Shah

œæ

LETTERS AND THE CHARITABLE KING

People are always asking why I correspond with them so seldom.
Here are two answers to that.

The first is that there was a king who asked a dervish why he
did not come to see him more often. The dervish answered:
'Because "Why have you not been here lately?" are sweeter to my
ears than "Why have you come again?".'

The second is that there was once a king who developed a
charitable outlook and decided to distribute all his wealth equally
among the people of the world. When all the necessitous ones had
been counted, however, it was discovered that there was no coin
small enough to give an equal amount to each: quite apart from the
fact that the smallest coin had by itself no purchasing power.

Merely to reproduce one's words and circulate them to all
interested people may appear to be keeping in touch with them:
but, unless the occasion is suitable, it is only of social value, not of
informative usefulness, let alone of knowledge value.

If we are to admit that it is strictly social needs which are
fulfilled by writings and meetings, then I will insist all the more
upon a proper social relationship, not a false one produced by
modern methods of multiplying copies.

HUMAN DEVELOPMENT

Many people imagine that any higher human development, if it
exists at all, must follow a pattern whose form (or at least whose
beginning) is instantly perceptible to them as such.

In making this assumption these people expose themselves to
control by any system which can take advantage of this expectation.
And systems do take advantage of this.

Many aspects of higher human development can only take the
form of communicating knowledge and experience in a disguised
manner: rather as we teach our children by involving them in

activities which they consider to be amusements rather than lessons in (say) counting, or co-ordination, or manners.

One method of accustoming people to a 'higher pattern' is to involve them in activities and enterprises which are equivalences of higher things.

Another procedure of great worth is also comparable to one employed in teaching children. It is to surround the pupil with data which he absorbs piecemeal until the 'penny drops'.

BROADCASTING

You may know people quite well, see them every day, live in the same house with them. No special prominence attaches in their minds to what you say or do: until they know that you are to appear on television. Then they rush home early from the office, not to see you in the house, but to see you saying the same things on television.

In the same way, people who would not dream of reading one of your books will huddle uncomfortably around a radio set to hear other people talking about it.

It is a sad lack in the culture not to have made it possible for people to take an interest in something unless it is dramatised (by the mere act of being broadcast) or ritualised.

It is the same with people who say: 'I must come to your lecture.' You say: 'You can hear me saying the same things every day, without coming to a meeting.' 'But it is not the same,' they say.

PRISON

Visualise a man who has to rescue people from a certain prison. It has been decided that there is only one promising way of carrying this out.

The rescuer has to get into the prison area without attracting attention. He must remain there relatively free to operate, for a certain period of time. The solution arrived at is that he shall enter it as a convict.

He accordingly arranges for himself to be apprehended and sentenced. Like others who have fallen foul of this particular machine in this manner, he is consigned to the prison which is his goal.

When he arrives he knows that he has been divested of any possible device which would help in an escape: All he has is his plan, his wits, his skills and his knowledge. For the rest, he has to make do with improvised equipment, acquired in the prison itself.

The major problem is that the inmates are suffering from a prison psychosis. This makes them think that their prison is the whole world. It is also characterised by selective amnesia of their past. Consequently they have hardly any memory of the existence, outline and detail of the world outside.

The history of our man's fellow-prisoners is prison history, their lives are prison lives. They think and act accordingly.

Instead of hoarding bread, for instance, as escape provisions, they mould it into dominoes with which they play games. Some of these games they know to be diversions, others they consider to be real. Rats, which they could train as a means of communication with the outside, they treat instead as pets. The alcohol in the cleaning-fluid available to them they drink to produce hallucinations, which delight them. They would think it sadly wasted, a crime, even, if anyone were to use it to drug the guards insensible, making escape possible.

The problem is aggravated because our malefactors have forgotten the various meanings of some of the ordinary words which we have been using. If you ask them for definitions of such words as 'provisions', 'journey', 'escape', even 'pets', this is the kind of list which you would elicit from them:

Provisions: prison food.

Journey: walking from one cell-block to another.

Escape: avoiding punishment by warders.

Pets: rats.

'The outside world' would sound to their ears like a bizarre contradiction in terms:

'As this is the world, this place where we live,' they would say, 'how can there be another one outside?'

The man who is working on the rescue plan can operate at first only by analogy.

There are few prisoners who will even accept his analogies, for they seem like mad babblings.

The babblings, when he says 'We need provisions for our journey of escape to the outside world,' of course sound to them like the following admitted nonsense:

'We need provisions – food for use in prison – for our journey – for walking from one cell-block to another – of escape – to avoid punishment by warders – to the outside world – to the prison outside . . . '

Some of the more serious-minded prisoners may say that they want to understand what he means. But they do not know outside-world language any more . . .

When this man dies, some of them make of his words and acts a prison-cult. They use it to comfort themselves, and to find arguments against the next liberator who manages to come among them.

A minority, however, do from time to time escape.

TESTING

There is a Persian proverb: 'To test that which has been tested is ignorance.'

To try to test something without the means of testing is even worse.

I KNOW THAT ALREADY

One of the commonest defences against really learning something is to believe that one knows it already.

If you say 'I know that!' when someone who knows your interests and how to teach says something, you are indulging in this almost unconscious activity.

WITHOUT COMMENT

I was invited one day to the home of a distinguished psychiatrist.

He received me in his study. There was another guest present.

While we were in the study this man talked very volubly. We went into another room to listen to some tape-recordings. The other guest interrupted them frequently with his opinions.

When dinner was served, the same man monopolised the conversation.

After the meal, he talked and talked over coffee in the drawing-room.

Eventually he left, and I stayed behind to finish some discussions with our host.

I said to him:

'That man talked a great deal in the study.'

'Yes,' said the psychiatrist, 'that was because he did not know you, and he was nervous.'

'But he talked a lot while we were playing the tapes.'

'Yes, that was because he felt that they were competition for him.'

'And he talked all through dinner.'

'Yes, that was because, with my wife present, he felt more at ease.'

'And then there was all that talk after dinner, while we were having coffee.'

'Yes, that was because the drawing-room was rather large for him, and he felt that he had to fill it with his voice to compensate.'

'I suppose that he would talk a great deal in a very small room, because he would feel hemmed in,' I said.

'Yes, that's a fair assumption,' said the psychiatrist.

COERCIVE AGENCIES

Make it your business to study in your life and in your surroundings:

The growth, development and activity of informal coercive agencies, not often recognised as such because of the poorly-delineated identification and measurement tools in current use.

Such tyrannies seldom have guns, clubs, centralised propaganda machines, uniforms and recognisable officials.

If you set up an experiment in any expectation, this expectation becomes a coercive agency whose attempts to lead you to certain conclusions you will have to take into account. Certain customs, social pressures, personal predilictions, even individual decisions, can become coercive agencies in your life.

One of the reasons why man struggles against what he takes to be undesirable is that he unconsciously recognises the coercive influences in the surroundings and in himself. He then chooses a measurable form of them, to satisfy and therefore 'abolish' his need to resist or frustrate them.

He has in so doing, of course, only begged the question.

Thoughts, circumstances, the social milieu, a hundred and one things, can provide as powerful coercive agencies as anything that the human being can point to as a 'despotism', or 'tyranny'.

If you are against tyranny, you must be against all tyranny in order to be consistent: not just an aunt-sally tyranny.

A set of misunderstood ideas or practises may become such a tyranny. A group of people who deal with each other with the greatest kindness yet who perform practises or carry out other activities unsuitable for their development are such an agency.

The tyranny of ideas or practises is far subtler and more effective than the avowed repressive institution because the participants are not aware that they are being constrained. The extreme case, the man who spends all his time shouting 'I'm free, I tell you!' is not free, because of lack of time, to do anything other than shout 'I'm free!'

Certain coercive agencies have become indispensable to the victims. People with closed minds or small ranges of thought and action depend for their pleasures upon the rewards offered by obedience to the coercive agency. If this obedience is couched in the form of 'disobedience', they feel that they are not coerced.

Such people cannot make progress towards their mental liberation at one bound. Their world has to be made larger, and to be seen to be larger, before they can take any step beyond their narrow life.

There is no repression like that of the man who causes his own, in the name of freeing himself. Since he cannot attribute it to any outside source, and since he cannot see himself suppressing himself, he may very well be lost. He is already under the duress of 'Slavery is freedom'. It is interestingly indicative of his state that he fears loss of freedom while he has already lost it. He does this because – like a child – if he has lost something and merely pretends that he might lose it, this implies that he has still got it.

We need not talk of social action, politics nor economics, nor even sociology in this matter. The individual, and groupings of people, have to learn that they cannot reform society in reality, nor deal with others as reasonable people, unless the individual has learned to locate and allow for the various patterns of coercive institutions, formal and also informal, which rule him. No matter what his reason says, he will always relapse into obedience to the coercive agency while its pattern is within him.

This is one reason why you see people converted from one system of belief or practise to another: they are aware of the shortcomings of the first; they can pretend that the second, because it does not have the outer defects to which he takes exception, is 'true', when the former was 'not true'.

The Study of Coercive Agencies and Man is what I would call this effort.

FORTUNE

'When Fortune knocks, open the door,' they say.

But why should one make fortune knock, by keeping the door shut?

A FEW SHORT MILES . . .

Have you ever noticed how much difference a few years or a few short miles, can make to something?

William Tell – the Swiss hero – so far as can be discovered, never existed. His tale, however, is found in Faridudin Attar's Bird Parliament. The Central Asian Haji Bektash, only a few miles from Turkey, becomes in the Balkans 'Hartschl Petesch'. The Ascension of Mohammed becomes the source for Dante.

Have you ever wondered, when you have heard that the 'Three Kings' of the Bible do not figure in the Bible at all, how some of the ideas which you cherish or are impressed by started their careers?

At least, in Japan, 'Tupiraita' is still applied to a typewriter, and 'smoking' is in France a dinner-jacket. But why should 'Dervish' become in English 'raving religious maniac'?

The value of this kind of literary exposition should be as much to show the warping of ideas as to correct the original definitions.

If you are aware of the deforming process itself, you will be able to escape it, not just to rely upon being fed the results of others' research. They may, you know, have missed things which could be important to you.

If the dervish teacher Turabi is so effective that even his garbled names become a totem (St Therapion), what happened to his original effectiveness? Do you want the totem or that which was of more than suggestive effect?

SAFE AND SORRY

'Better to be safe than to be sorry' is a remark of value only when these are the actual alternatives.

IDOLS

Have you noticed how economical the human race is with its idols?

It sets them up, enjoys them, then falls upon them and devours them until there is nothing left.

Even the complete consumption of the idol, if it is another human being, is not the end. There are then hundreds of years' worth of argument and analysis to be worked through.

PROMISES

Never promise, even by implication, without fulfilling your promise.

The only acceptable alternative to completing an undertaking is to over-fulfil it.

To betray any promise, explicit or otherwise, will harm you more than it can harm anyone else.

SYSTEMS OF KNOWLEDGE

No system is any use if you merely possess it. Ownership requires operation.

No system is useful if one can only experiment with it. For a system to be useful, it must be correctly operated.

The means of operating a system must correspond with contemporary needs. It should not be imitatively traditionalistic.

Defectiveness of a system should not be confused with human shortcomings. People cannot attain certain things unless they have the means.

A system may be complete for one set of circumstances, defective for another.

Possession of a system, or any part of it, or an interest in it or in discovering one, should not be assumed to confer any license or capacity, to operate it.

Individual criticisms of a system, incapacity to operate it, or dissatisfaction with it should not be confused with any shortcoming of the system.

Consistency in a system, like inconsistency, is always more apparent than real: because what is coherent in one frame of reference may not be so in another.

These points are intended to emphasise that information and familiarisation with a system are much more important, vital and urgent than to apply existing imaginings about it to any attempt to understand or operate it.

Experience comes before understanding and before capacity to operate.

OCCASION

Every part of your development as a human being needs correct time, right place, suitable company.

Without these you will be as complete as anything else which lacks three desirable elements in due concert: like a plant, say, without water, sun and earth.

BIAS

'Rather the bias of the sympathetic human than the obstinate justice of the ass.'

Better still the removal of bias.

A bias towards 'goodness' is still a bias.

The ass of justice has a bias towards 'justice'.

The unbiased has no need of bias: he has knowledge.

Principles and inelastic rules are the last bastion of the primitive. Principles are guides which substitute for knowledge; rules are drawn up to guide those who do not know.

Primitive man has stayed with us for aeons, sustained by the pessimist belief that, since knowledge is impossible, substitutes must always be employed instead.

A substitute is, however, to be used only when the real thing is not available.

If too long deprived of the genuine article, man starts to demand only the substitute. That demand, however, does not convert the substitute into the real thing.

Sufficient and sufficiently sustained adulation of the substitute and it becomes the aim of the seeker. Ignoring the existence of the real thing, and even its possibility, is as effective in abolishing it as if it were not there, for practical purposes.

This is why men of knowledge must not only exist: they have to represent the very existence of knowledge, sometimes initially on a very low level.

Beware of people who say: 'We must have bias, even if it is bias towards good.' The fact is that we must have bias towards knowledge: for it is only knowledge which will destroy bias.

FAME AND MONEY

At the present time, fame – without diminution – can be turned into money.

Money can also be turned into fame, but not on the same terms.

A MOTTO OF THE HUMAN RACE

Tell me what to do; but it must be what I want you to tell me.

GENERAL GORDON

The story is told of a celebrated statue of General Gordon mounted upon a camel which was one of the sights of Khartoum.

This statue became a great favourite with a three-year-old boy, and his nursemaid used to take him every day as part of his walk, to 'see General Gordon'.

The day came when the family was leaving the Sudan, and the nurse took the little boy to say goodbye to General Gordon.

He stood for a long time looking at the statue, and said: 'I shall not be seeing you again for a long time, so goodbye General Gordon.'

Then he turned from the man on the camel to the young woman and said to her:

'Nanny, who is that sitting on General Gordon's back?'

This tale could very well be true. It illustrates as well as would any other the manner in which people assume things about knowledge without ever imagining that their view may be inconsistent with real circumstances. Sometimes it is almost by accident, as in this case, that one knows exactly what it is that the person has seen awry, although it may be evident that he is not clear about it.

Like the camel of General Gordon, people often imagine that the means of transportation of a teaching is the teaching itself. For this reason they carry on revering the externals of individuals, or mere words, or exercises or theories. What counts is the effect, not the appearance, of a thing.

Like our little boy, the student may see something which prompts him to ask a question which could clear everything up. And the information that he has been attached to something in the name of something else may be unwelcome.

DEAD AND ALIVE

It is a pity that there is a taboo which prevents us from investigating it, but the fact is, nevertheless:

A lot of people who are clinically, intellectually and emotionally alive actually died in every other sense years ago.

People are afraid of taking this line of thought in case they turn out to be one of these: so they say that such a conception is ridiculous.

They need not bother themselves, because if they are such as I have mentioned, they will never find it out.

JUDGEMENT

Make sure, before you judge anything that what seems to you to be untrue, most unlikely, unworthy of your consideration – is not in fact what you need. Everybody's truth is at some time someone else's untruth.

GOOD AND BAD

Don't call anyone 'good' or 'bad' until you have covertly observed him.

With a long enough run, or a sufficiently permissive environment, you can see much of what he is really like.

This knowledge, however, carries no license to oppose him.

THOUGHT

A great deal of thought is only a substitute for the thoughts which the individual would really find useful at the time.

WORDS AND INFORMATION

Words are more often used to conceal information than to convey it.

People who try the hardest to communicate, or think that they do, are generally preventing communication.

DEMONSTRATION

Do you want to examine a socially-conditioned individual who attributes what has been done to him as the work of a higher power?

All you need to do is to look at nine out of ten 'dedicated' people.

GOOD

Show me a man who thinks that he knows what 'good' is, and I will probably be able to show you a horror of a person.

Show me a person who really knows what 'good' is, and I will show you that he almost never uses the word.

MAN

Kick him – he'll forgive you. Flatter him – he may or may not see through you.

But ignore him, and he'll hate you, even if he conceals it until he dies.

POLITENESS AND TRUTH

Politeness and telling the truth are, to your certain knowledge as well as mine, often opposites.

Any society which enjoins its members to adhere to both of these is a fraud.

All sorts of compromise formulae have been devised to gloss over or obscure this basic weakness. It remains nonetheless.

This is not an exhortation to abandon politeness or telling the truth. It is a statement which has to be carefully thought about.

THE EFFORT BEHIND A TEACHING

Ordinary individuals reared on incomplete information, have no conception of the amount of work which precedes the appearance and grafting operations of a great historical event.

It is not surprising, therefore, though invariably inconvenient, that they expect immediate and miraculous happenings, successes, movements.

They triumph in the end, of course, because it is they who write the history, the hagiography, the exegetics.

STRUCTURE OF A SYSTEM

Observe an authority-figure, an 'eternally valid literature', a hierarchy, commands and prohibitions.

Do you know what you are seeing, apart from what its name may be?

You are looking at the structure of a conditioning system. No higher usefulness is manifested at such a level.

For a higher usefulness to be obtained, it may be sought apart from externals. Attachment to totems, slogans and mandarins can only inhibit this process, however useful these appurtenances might be for other purposes.

ILLUSTRATION CONFUSED WITH BELIEF

One of the tragedies of modern times is that people have come to believe that something said by someone in the past, perhaps for illustrative or provocation purposes, actually represents that person's beliefs at the time.

WORK

If you call different things by the same name, you start confusion.

If you call 'work' every kind of labour, you are doing this.

If you are working below capacity, you are not working.

If you are working at something you cannot do, you are not working.

If you are working with enjoyment, without it, for necessity, and so on, you are able to only use the one word, 'work' and hence you are inefficient at describing what you are doing.

TIME

People complain about time being short, going fast.

But when it seems to go slowly they complain that it drags.

Let us consider the people, not the supposed movements of time.

TEACHING

Please do not start to teach the blind until you have practised living with closed eyes.

VIRTUES

Ethic is socially conditioned. Human virtue is not the same as that of another sphere. Sometimes, however, the two run parallel.

RESTRAINT

The original purpose of cultivating restraint is so that eventually one will not need to have restraint.

KNOWLEDGE

How curious that a man who closes his hand upon air so often thinks that he has a ruby within his grasp.

INNER KNOWLEDGE

You want to become wise in one lesson:

First become a real human being.

MEDITATION

Before you learn how to meditate, you must unlearn what you think meditation might be.

INTELLECTUALS

The self-styled intellectual sneers at the humble man's respect for some things.

But if you want to see stupidity clearly and have a firework show into the bargain, speak against the thinkers' sacred cows.

You are then more likely to have a demonstration of what 'raving like a maniac' means.

FOUR SEEKERS

The chief of one band of seekers found a book. He and his followers studied it, forgetting that a means was not an end.

In another case the leader of a collection of dervishes found some wool. They spent years in working with wool.

The guide of yet another circle discovered the virtues of plants, and instructed his companions in plant-lore.

The successor of a certain teacher, having absorbed only wood-working knowledge, instructed his students in this.

All worked with their materials. The book was memorised, and an attempt was made to apply its principles to everyday life. The wool was spun and made into yarn. The plants were cultivated and yielded dye. The wood was made into a variety of different artefacts.

Then came a man of knowledge. He called together all the scattered groupings, and said to them:

'You have the materials. Now I will show you how, with your experience and my knowledge, a carpet may be made.'

But few could detach from wool, from wood, from plants and from book upon book.

Those few became the carpet-makers.

So it is with Sufi knowledge. Combining the parts make the whole. But the people of wood want to work with wood. This would be well enough if there were a market for wood.

WHAT, AND FROM WHOM?

Do you expect milk from a bee, honey from a chicken, or eggs from a cow?

These ideas are absurd. Yet how many people stop, before they ask for information and guidance from people who do not know, that they are asking the impossible?

The reason why they do not stop to think is essentially that they are not seeking information, knowledge, guidance. They are asking to be entertained, to pass the time, to be given attention.

This is the reason why, as we have all experienced, people will ask for advice often enough, but do not take it, however good it may be. The purpose of the transaction is not to seek advice.

And this is a reason why Sufis are often not popular. Since it is not necessarily any part of their duty to carry on disguised therapies, they may not co-operate in the fiction: and people do not like that at all.